PRACTICING
for Young Musicians

You Are Your Own Teacher

PRACTICING
for Young Musicians
You Are Your Own Teacher

REVISED & EXPANDED EDITION

by

Harvey R. Snitkin, Ph.D.

hmp
PUBLICATIONS INC.

NIANTIC, CONNECTICUT

Cover and text design by Mary Ballachino

Publisher's Cataloging-in-Publication

Snitkin, Harvey R.
     Practicing for young musicians : you are your own teacher / Harvey R. Snitkin. -- Rev. and expanded ed.
          p.   cm.
     Includes index.
     Preassigned LCCN: 96-94279
     ISBN 1-888732-00-8
     1. Musical instruments--Instruction and study.   2. Practicing (Music).
     I. Title.
MT170.S65   1996
780'.68—dc20

                                                            781.44
                                                        QBI96-40270

Manufactured in the United States of America
Revised Edition/Third Printing

Acknowledgments

I would like to thank my students, over the past thirty years, for sharing their needs with me, and giving me the reason for writing this book, Allyn Donath for reading and making valuable comments on an early manuscript draft, Corinne Weber for her editorial advice, Mary Ballachino, of Merrimac Design, for her attention to design details, and my wife Michele for her advice about final design and editorial decisions.

I would also like to thank Armstrong Woodwinds; D'Addario and Company, Inc.; Electronic Courseware Systems, Inc.; Fender Musical Instruments; Franz Manufacturing Company; Hamilton Stands Inc.; Harmonic Vision; Hohner, Inc.; Homespun Tapes; Interworld Music; Leblanc Corporation; Mark of the Unicorn; Pure-Cussion Inc.; Steinway and Sons; The Getzen Company; The Selmer Company, Inc.; Twelve Tone Systems, Inc.; United Musical Instruments U.S.A., Inc.; Weber Reeds; and Yamaha Audio, Guitar, and Synthesizer for supplying black and white photographs, transparencies and disks used to highlight and illustrate the text.

I regret that space did not allow for the use of all the materials so generously submitted by the manufacturers. The sources of photographs used are acknowledged individually in the photo credits.

I would especially like to thank Virgil Maines, President of Hamilton Stands Incorporated, for supplying the stands used for the cover photograph.

And, a special thank you to my wife Michele and daughters Dale and Marla for their patience and for listening when I discussed the book at inappropriate times.

"... a minor masterpiece of motivation, encouragement and self-help ... the tone light, and the humor refreshing."
Richard White, *The Post Road Review*

"... a book music teachers will want to recommend to their students, and parents will want to purchase along with their child's chosen instrument."
The Nashville News, Nashville, IL

"... this book should be given to every family whose child takes up an instrument. It should be mandatory reading."
Tony Mazzarella, winner of "Parents' Choice" award.

"This lighthearted book requires no prior musical background, yet the concepts are not watered down."
Houston Tribune, Houston, TX

"... an excellent text on self-practice and self-teaching techniques, and an excellent addition to the instructional tools of the trade."
Connecticut Songsmith,
the Connecticut Songwriters Association

"... a unique holistic approach to keep young, beginning music students interested and enthused."
Norwich Bulletin, Norwich, CT

This book ... will make practicing an enjoyable topic."
The Freer Press, Freer, TX

"... ingenious and very helpful. "
Victor Norman, Conductor Emeritus,
Eastern Connecticut Symphony Orchestra

Contents

Preface

Wouldn't it be great to say, "I want to practice!" instead of "I have to practice?," and mean it?

Why shouldn't practicing be as exciting as earning an "A" or hitting a home run? Unfortunately, that's not always the case. Practicing is too often discussed only when it hasn't been done. Then, the conversation ends with, "Gee, do I have to practice?"

The purpose of this book is to help you change "I have to practice" to "I want to practice." It is meant to help you understand why you're practicing, what you hope to accomplish through practicing and by letting the power of music guide you.

Music is a powerful form of communication. Without cables or a telephone, you can express and share feelings and not speak a word. You can explore the feelings of people living today and share the feelings of those who lived throughout history.

History is fascinating. History books, however, can only tell you where people lived, how they lived and what they did. But only music, and the arts, can keep you in touch with *how* they felt.

Let music be your passport to exploring the past, understanding the present and creating the future. Practicing will build the skills needed to plan your trip.

Every time you practice, you're taking another step on a musical journey that will last a lifetime. Learning to perform, listen to and create music will provide the transportation. I hope that this book will provide a road map and help you explore the landscape.

Have a wonderful trip!

Harvey Snitkin

How to Use this Book

If you are currently studying a musical instrument, or are planning to study one, this book is for you. This book is not only for you—it's your book.

It won't be yours, however, if you browse through it and put it aside. When you practice you take action. Do the same with this book. Read it through to get the broad picture of what practicing is about. Then take action! Read it again. As you find helpful hints, underline them, highlight them, write notes to yourself in the margin or in the space provided at the end of each part. Try to incorporate these ideas into your practice sessions.

Re-read this book periodically; the ideas and analogies will take on new meaning as you progress.

Take another action. Lend it to your parents.

Parents, if your son or daughter hasn't lent you this book, ask if you can borrow it. It will help you understand why they're practicing, and what they hope to accomplish through it. After reading the book, discuss practicing with them.

Make practicing something else you share. Your interest and understanding is your child's most important motivation. Anything you share can only help strengthen a relationship.

Then, lend this book to their teachers.

Teachers know that each child is unique and that all children will grow by accepting responsibility for their progress. This book relates practicing to daily life and supplies analogies that will be helpful in explaining to students the "whats" and "whys" of practicing.

Throughout this book, young musicians are told, "The way you think is the way you play or sing," and that "during lessons you are renting your teacher's ears." Therefore, teachers should keep in mind that the way they teach is the way their students practice.

In short, let this book open a healthy three way dialogue among students, parents and teachers. A healthy dialogue will make practicing a positive and rewarding topic, not a negative one that's only discussed when it hasn't been done.

A Note About the Musical Examples

This book is for all young musicians, regardless of the instrument they play or the voice part they sing. To accommodate all readers, musical examples relating to scales and music reading are provided in three clefs, treble, bass and alto. Musical examples, however, that illustrate concepts and general topics (sustained sound, articulation, etc.) are given in one clef. The readers can supply the clef appropriate for their instrument or voice.

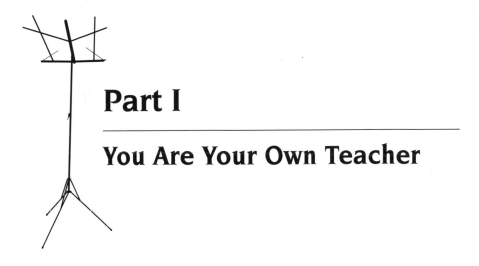

Part I

You Are Your Own Teacher

Introduction

The New Arrival Part One

"It's a boy!" It's a girl!" Those three words gave your parents one of the happiest days of their lives, a day they still celebrate—your birthday.

When you were born, however, you weren't born with an owner's manual. You didn't pop into the world, book in hand, and say, "O.K. here I am! Here's my operator's guide. You want to keep me healthy, read Chapter Two. And oh yeah, happy—that's important—be sure to read Chapter Seven. In fact, if you read this manual from cover to cover, I'll be practically trouble free."

That would've been convenient, but it's not the way it was. Your parents learned how to be parents by trial and error. They learned how to be parents because suddenly they had to *think* like parents.

They added something new to their lives—you. Building the relationship you now enjoy is the result of their time, caring and patience.

The New Arrival Part Two

In many ways, the day your new instrument arrives is the same. You look at a shiny trumpet, saxophone, flute, violin, drum, guitar, piano or synthesizer and think of all the things you can do together.

Now you have to take the time and patience to build a caring relationship with your new instrument. Your new instrument will change your life. The relationship that develops is now up to you.

To build that relationship, you'll spend a great deal of time practicing. But, building any relationship takes time. The way you spend that time determines the kind of relationship you build.

Most of your practicing will provide satisfaction and musical growth. At times, however, it will be frustrating. When that happens, remember, developing a good relationship also takes patience and understanding. But, as your parents will tell you, building a good relationship is worth the effort!

That's what this book is about—building a good relationship with your instrument and using the time you spend with it to assure the friendliest and most rewarding relationship possible.

1

A Little Help
from Some Friends

Backwards Bob was a good baseball player. He could hit, he could catch and he could throw. Running the bases was Backwards' problem. Bob went to see the baseball coach at school. The coach showed him how to run the bases correctly, gave him some hints on how to do it faster and told Backwards to come back in a week.

Backwards practiced all week. Hour after hour. He even used a stopwatch to keep track of his progress.

The following week Bob returned. He stood at home plate, swung the bat and ran with lightning speed around the base paths. The coach was shocked! Good old Backwards did it again. He ran to third base, then to second base, on to first base and back to home plate. The coach could only smile and tell Backwards Bob what he had done wrong.

Perfect Patricia, on the other hand, could be given directions and follow them, paying attention to every detail. Patricia's home economics assignment was to make a skirt.

As her teacher directed, she went to the store, bought a pattern, took it home and read the instructions. Then she laid out the cloth, pinned the pattern to it and cut along the dotted lines. Finally, she sewed the skirt together.

The skirt was perfect, just the right color and style. Patricia ran to her room and put it on so she could show it to her parents. To her alarm, she couldn't button it. The skirt was too small!

Worrisome Walt was a nervous wreck whenever he studied for tests. No one could understand why tests upset him. He understood the material and worked hard at his studies.

Unfortunately, Walt couldn't concentrate. Every time he took a test, he worried. "What if I don't get a good grade? My parents will be angry, maybe they won't let me go out with my friends. They might even take away my bike, my video games, the television, or worse, my allowance."

With all this going on in Worrisome Walt's head, he never did as well as he should have. When tests were returned, he was always angry with himself. Although he knew the correct answers, he couldn't get them from his mind to the paper when he needed them.

Happy Harry was just the opposite. He was always fun to be with. Never a dull moment with Happy Harry. He had confidence in his sense of humor even if he didn't always work as hard as he should have. He would always try to joke his way out of embarrassing situations.

If Happy Harry lived by any philosophy, it was: "When in

doubt, pun!" Like the time Harry's history teacher asked him why George Washington never told a lie. Harry smiled and said, "George Washington's teeth were false, but his tongue wasn't." His teacher smiled and thought, "That's Harry."

Who Would Make the Best Musician?

If Backwards Bob, Perfect Patricia, Worrisome Walt and Happy Harry were to study a musical instrument, which one do you think would do the best? Taking another look at them as musicians, who would you vote for?

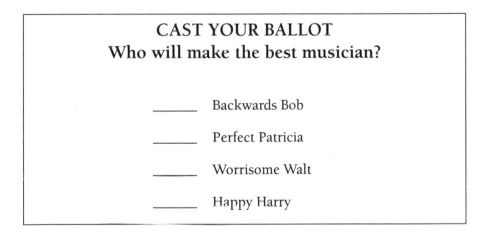

CAST YOUR BALLOT
Who will make the best musician?

_____ Backwards Bob

_____ Perfect Patricia

_____ Worrisome Walt

_____ Happy Harry

Backwards Bob?

Backwards Bob may not be as backwards as he seems. He knew what he wanted to improve and he worked hard at it. With his determination, he'll do fine when he learns to run in the right direction.

Perfect Patricia?

If you said Perfect Patricia would make the best musician, you might be right. To play a musical instrument, you certainly have to follow directions and pay attention to detail. Perfect Patricia would practice all her scales and exercises, and probably learn to play the notes quickly and accurately. She might forget, however, that being a musician means putting yourself into the music. She might also forget that the reason for studying a musical instrument is to play music: to use the instrument to express your feelings and to share those feelings with others. If you don't put yourself into the music, all the correct notes and rhythms, like the materials that went into making the skirt, will not guarantee a perfect fit.

Worrisome Walt?

Worrisome Walt, like Backwards Bob, is hard working and would practice diligently. Worrisome Walt, however, might also forget something. He might forget that his music gives him another means for expressing his feelings. But first, Walt must try to understand his true feelings. He shouldn't try to feel the way he thinks others want him to feel. What's important is what Walt gets from his music. Worrisome will do well when he "lets himself do well."

Happy Harry?

Happy Harry's outlook is different. He enjoys everything, especially a good joke and a good laugh. If Harry had a musical philosophy, it would be: "If you make a mistake, make a LOUD one." With Harry's confidence, he could be a fine musician if he worked at it.

His happy-go-lucky personality would come through in his music. Music will give Happy Harry, as it will Backwards Bob, Perfect Patricia and Worrisome Walt, another way of expressing his personality.

The Votes Are In

As you can see, Backwards Bob, Perfect Patricia, Worrisome Walt and Happy Harry could all make good musicians. Each has special qualities to bring to their music. It takes the hard work of a Backwards Bob and a Worrisome Walt, the ability to concentrate on detail of a Perfect Patricia, and the confidence of self-expression of a Happy Harry to be a good musician.

We can learn some important points about practicing from our four friends. From Walt and Harry we learn that what we do depends on how we think—our attitude. When it comes to playing a musical instrument, you could even say, "The way you think is the way you play." From Bob and Patricia we learn that what we accomplish depends on how we apply the instruction we receive.

Our four friends have also taught us the two important, but usually overlooked, truths about practicing:

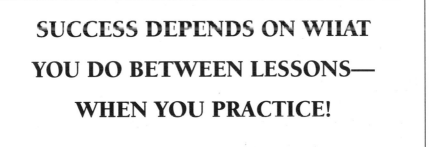

SUCCESS DEPENDS ON WHAT
YOU DO BETWEEN LESSONS—
WHEN YOU PRACTICE!

— AND —

BETWEEN LESSONS, YOU ARE YOUR OWN TEACHER!

To practice and be your own teacher, however, first you'll have to understand what practicing is, and what teachers do.

2

Some Thoughts About Practicing

Practicing Is a Commitment

You can accomplish anything you want once you make a commitment to yourself to develop the needed skills and knowledge.

Practicing is that type of commitment. You make a commitment to yourself to improve by developing skills from lesson to lesson. To develop new skills, you'll go over and over them until they become a useful part of your musical vocabulary. You're as much of a "doer" practicing music as you are when practicing baseball or studying for tests.

Practice Can Make "Perfect" or "Imperfect"

Any time you do something repeatedly, however, you develop habits. That sounds simple enough, except that the habits you develop can be good or bad. The old expression "practice makes perfect" refers only to good habits. When bad habits develop, practice can also make "imperfect."

Poor Backwards Bob! No one could say he wasn't committed! He practiced hard. Unfortunately, he taught himself a new habit—a bad one. Now when he plays baseball, softball or kickball, he runs even slower than before. He has to think about which direction to run. Running in the right direction feels uncomfortable.

What went wrong with his practicing? He started with the right idea, found a problem and attempted to correct it. Unfortunately, he used the wrong rules of the game. He developed a new skill that hurt rather than helped his baseball playing. The more he practiced, the more of a habit it became. Now he has to work twice as hard, first to unlearn the bad habit and then to relearn the good one. If he had run in the right direction at the start, he would've developed a good habit the first time.

You're the Player and the Umpire

The nice part about the "practice game" is that you make the rules for yourself. You're the player and the umpire. You judge good from bad. Understand your rules, and run in the right direction the first time. Why get frustrated breaking bad habits when developing good habits is less work and more fun?

To Be a Musician, Think Like a Musician

Backwards Bob practiced base running because he wanted to be a better baseball player. But, unfortunately, Bob didn't think like a baseball player. The object of the game isn't how fast you can run bases, but to run the base paths to score runs. Bob could be a good baseball player once he learns to think like a baseball player.

The same is true for Bob, the musician. Bob practices his instrument to play music—to be a musician. To be successful as a musician, he'll have to think like a musician.

Practicing Makes Skills Automatic

Baseball teams have batting practice, infield practice and outfield practice. Players try to improve each part of their game at every practice session. When these skills are needed in a game situation, they're automatic. Players don't think about skills, they just use them.

Musical practice sessions are no different. You practice scales, exercises, rhythms, finger control, breath, bow, pick, stick control and other techniques. When these skills are needed, they're automatic. You don't have to think about skills, you just use them.

When the musical game requires them, you're ready: ready for a great game that lets you be an individual or a member of a team.

Even Good Games Can Get Dull

Remember the time Happy Harry dressed up as the principal and told three teachers to stay after school for not doing their homework? Well, it was funny the first time, but the same joke soon became a dull game. The practice game, like Harry's joke, can also become dull. For an exciting game, you start with a purpose and end with a sense of satisfaction.

If the rules lose their spark, so does the game. If the rules remain challenging, so does the game. The game rules you establish for yourself determine what skills you practice and why you're practicing them.

Spend Your Practice Time Wisely: It's Simple Addition

Perfect Patricia might say that practicing is like a math problem. A problem in addition may or may not be fun as a homework assignment. If, however, you use the same numbers to add up the money you've saved, the same problem takes on a new meaning. The excitement isn't attached to the numbers, but to the ways you can enjoy spending the money. You can waste it or spend it wisely.

One of the most precious things you have costs nothing, yet it's priceless—TIME. Wasting your time is like wasting your money. What does this have to do with practicing? The excitement comes from time well spent. You choose how to spend your practice time just as you choose how to spend your money.

When you decide how to spend your money, you have decisions to make. If you buy something you've wanted, it leads to enjoyment and satisfaction.

When you decide how to spend your practice time you also have decisions to make. Practice time well spent will also lead to enjoyment and satisfaction: the enjoyment of being able to do something at the end of a practice session that you couldn't do at the beginning, and the satisfaction of challenging yourself to improve a little each day.

HOMEWORK ASSIGNMENT
Which sounds like more fun?

What is the sum of:

	$2.60
	$3.50
	$4.00
	$10.10

I've Saved:

$2.60 in dimes and nickels
$3.50 in quarters
$4.00 in one dollar bills
$10.10

Decision:

"Is the sum correct?"

Decision:

"What is the most enjoyable
way to spend $10.10?"

Between Lessons, You Are Your Own Teacher!

Real progress happens when you take your weekly lesson. Right? Wrong! It is true that lessons are rewarding. That's when new skills are introduced. Success, however, depends on how you work on those skills between lessons, when you practice. And, between lessons, You Are Your Own Teacher!

It's Simple Mathematics

Worrisome Walt might think, "That's ridiculous, I can't be the teacher—I'm me, the student."

Perfect Patricia, however, would say, "It's simple mathematics. If you practice one hour a day, you'd practice seven hours a week. But your lesson is probably a half hour. Seven hours are broken into fourteen half hours. That means you spend fourteen times as much time practicing each week than you do at your lesson. During those

---

**IF YOU PRACTICE ONE HOUR A DAY
AND TAKE A HALF HOUR WEEKLY LESSON,
YOU SPEND:**

7 Hours practicing = 14 half hours

½ Hour lesson = ½ hour

*You spend 14 times as much time practicing each week
as you do in your lesson.*

practice sessions you take over where your teacher left off. You, and your ears, become your teacher."

Your Ears Have a Long Reach

Believe it or not, you play or sing with your ears. Although Happy Harry might chuckle, "I'd play with my ears, but they won't reach the keys!" Harry is wrong. Your ears do reach the keys. They allow your thoughts to tell your hands, fingers, arms or breath what to do.

At Lessons, You Rent Your Teacher's Ears

Think about what happens during your lesson. Your teacher listens to you (play or sing). For that half hour, you're renting your teacher's ears! Teachers have developed sensitivity to sound through listening, practicing, studying and applying those skills over the years. Like your doctor, who diagnoses your health problems and gives you a prescription if you need one, your teacher diagnoses your playing or singing and makes suggestions.

Teachers listen and compare what they hear to how they think it should sound. Then you're complimented on what you did well, suggestions are made on what needs improvement and new skills are introduced. In short, you've rented your teacher's ears.

```
MR. SMITH'S MUSIC STUDIO

EARS FOR RENT!
```

When You Practice, Your Ears Become Your Teacher

After your lesson, you take over. You practice. Your success now depends on how good a teacher you are, and how well you develop your ears.

You play or sing, and like your teacher, you listen and compare what you hear to how you think it should sound. You give yourself a pat on the back for what you did well and decide what needs more work. By doing so, you improve on older skills and work in the new skills introduced at your last lesson.

Between lessons, practicing is challenging because you have the satisfaction of teaching yourself. You guide your own progress! You, and your ears, make your practice sessions worthwhile. Most of all, you and your ears pave the way to making your next lesson an opportunity for progress.

Concept of Sound: Your Practice Room Upstairs

Can You Taste It?

Think chocolate cake! Think of that creamy frosting on your lips! Is it good? Can you almost taste the chocolate cake by just thinking about it? What did you taste? Perfect Patricia might say that she tasted just the right mix of eggs, milk, flour, sugar and the other ingredients that went into the cake. Did you, or did you simply taste chocolate cake?

Now listen to a piece of music. Did you hear fingers moving, performers thinking, breathing, counting, reading music, putting instruments to their mouths, holding their bows, sticks or picks? Did you, or did you simply hear music?

If you think about chocolate cake enough, you can almost taste it. Why? Because you've probably eaten chocolate cake many times. You've memorized the flavor. If you baked a chocolate cake, you'd probably judge it by how it tasted compared to how you expected it to taste. You had a concept, a mental image, of the taste.

Developing a concept, or mental image, for the sound of musical instruments is no different. In time, you develop a taste for how you expect your instrument to sound, and how you expect music performed on it to sound, a taste for what you consider to be good tone quality and what isn't and a taste for what sounds musical and what doesn't.

Your Practice Room Upstairs

As your own teacher, your concepts of sound and musicianship become your practice room upstairs. If you think of everything you have to do with your mind and body to play a musical instrument, you'd drive yourself crazy! Yet, to get good tone quality (one that is pleasing) and good intonation (correct pitch levels), you have to do all the little things correctly. By listening to yourself and comparing what you hear to how you think it should sound, you can judge the progress of the smaller details.

Listening Is the Key to Developing a Concept of Sound

First, listen as you rent your teacher's ears. Become sensitive to what your teacher hears in your performance and try to remember the sounds that went along with various comments.

Listen to CDs and tapes. Listen to live performances by professionals and friends. Listen and evaluate what you hear. Listen and sing what you hear. The more you listen, the more you sing, the more you'll discover what you like and what you don't like, what kind of tone quality you like and what kind you don't like, a good performance and one that wasn't.

Your Concept of Sound Has Kept You Safe

If you think that developing a concept of sound is difficult, it isn't. You've used your ears to identify different sounds all your life. By learning to identify small differences in tone quality, you've remained safe. The sound of a car, or thunder, the bark of an angry dog, the whine of a siren, for example, warn you of danger.

You can pick up the telephone and recognize people on the other end by the sound (tone quality) of their voices. By recognizing changes in the tone qualities of their voices, you recognize changes in their moods.

The same is true of different performers on the same instrument. Performers can develop a tone quality that is as unique as their speaking voice, and through their tone quality they communicate changes in their moods.

To develop your musical voice, open your ears to the sounds around you, and consult your musical memory. It lives in your mind—in the practice room upstairs.

Helpful Hints from Old Friends

Before going on to Part II, Methods of Practicing, here are some helpful hints from old friends:

"Do your best. That is all anyone can expect from you. Everybody is unique and has a great deal to bring to their music. It is what you get from your involvement with music that is important. However, remember music is feelings, and any feelings of tension will be reflected in your playing or singing. Relax! Let yourself go and have fun. At times this is easier said than done!"

Best wishes,

Worrisome Walt

"The way you think is the way you play or sing, so be a thinking performer. We all learn from our mistakes, but if we can't hear them, we can't correct them. Listen to yourself and be sure you know what you want to correct and why before you just jump in and do it."

Have a good game,

Backwards Bob

"Have confidence in yourself. IF YOU MAKE A MISTAKE, MAKE A GOOD ONE! Everyone enjoys something funny! Laugh with yourself. If you make a sound that's funny, then laugh; just because it came out of your instrument doesn't make it any less humorous. If there is a single musical tone that should guide you it's B NATURAL."

Keep smiling,

Happy Harry

"If you are a thinking person, you will have questions. No question is foolish. Answers to your questions can set you on the right track and save months of wasted practice time. Write down questions so you will not forget them. UNCERTAINTY WILL NOT BUILD CONFIDENCE. WITH GOOD PRACTICE HABITS, STEADY PROGRESS IS AT YOUR FINGERTIPS."

Sincerely,

Perfect Patricia

Can You Guess?

Question: What do practicing and the instruments on the following pages have in common?

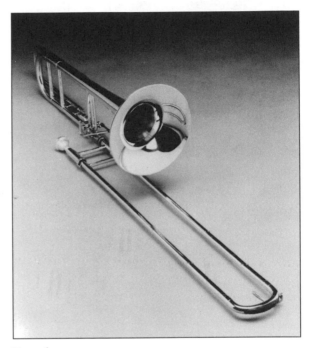

Trombone

Piccolos

Accordion

Tenor saxophone, alto saxophone   French horn

Grand piano

Oboe

Baritone horn

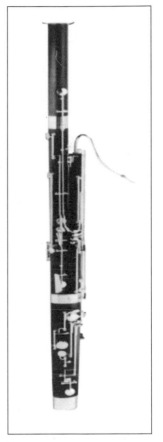

Trumpet

Bassoon

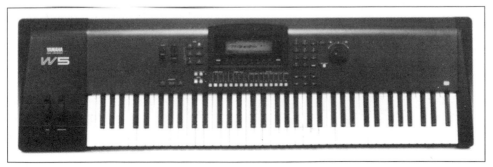

Synthesizer

Harmonica

Clarinet

Drum set

Violin

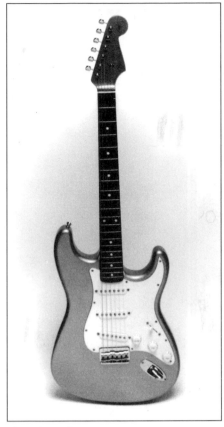

Electric guitar

Marching mellophone

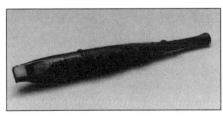

Song flute

Answer: Regardless of what instrument you play, or what style of music you hope to perform, the practice methods and concepts in the remainder of this book are the same!

Notes

Practicing Is a Commitment

You should listen to it your body is telling you what to play or its your own ears!

Part II

Planning Your Musical Travel: Ideas for an Enjoyable Trip

3

Planning Ahead: Your Road Map to Progress

"Are we there yet?" "How much longer?" How many times have you asked those questions on trips? Traveling is fun, but the real excitement starts when you arrive.

You wouldn't take a trip without knowing where you were going, or why you were going there. If you did, travel wouldn't be enjoyable. It would be tense, not knowing if you were on the right road or lost. You'd have no way of knowing if you were getting closer to your destination, or when you've arrived.

Yet that's the way some people practice, not knowing what they want to accomplish or when they've accomplished it. That's not practicing, that's putting in time.

Practice with a Destination in Mind

Planning practice sessions and planning a trip are similar. You decide where you want to go, and each landmark tells you when you are getting closer. Reaching your destination is the purpose of travel. Reaching your musical goals is the purpose of practicing. Practice with a destination in mind, and whether your trip is long (one hour) or short (5 minutes), begin with a purpose and end with a sense of arrival.

Take Your Mind Along for the Ride

"Wow! I'm going to the Grand Canyon!" Congratulations, you decided where you want to go. But you can't go alone. You have to take your mind along for the ride. Once you decide where you want to go, you're saying, "I'll move my body from here to there." But if you leave your mind at home, your body might get lost. You use your body to get from one place to another, and your mind to be sure you know where you're going.

Concentration:
The Secret of Not Getting Lost

Like traveling, practicing also requires both mental and physical effort. Concentration is the secret to not getting lost. Know what you want to accomplish in each practice session and concentrate on it. When you lose concentration, your mind wanders. Although you're going through the motions, your real practicing has stopped.

Backwards Bob would agree that time in itself may not accomplish what you want. It is what you do in that time that's important. Each minute spent with a definite purpose will bring you closer to your destination of gaining technical skills and musicianship. Each minute of "mindless drilling," however, may put you on the wrong road. Ask Backwards Bob! The bad habits you develop could even stop you from reaching your destination.

4

Decisions, Decisions, Always Decisions

Many decisions have to be made before planning a trip. The first, of course, is where will you go? Once that decision is made, you can consider others. How will you get there: by bicycle, car, train, boat or plane? What will you do? How long will you stay? What will you pack? How much money will you need?

There are also basic decisions to make before you can plan practice sessions. Consider some of the following. They'll make your musical journey more enjoyable and productive.

When Should I Practice?

You wouldn't plan a trip without checking your calendar for the best time to travel. You might want to know: "When is school vacation?" "What have I already told friends I would do with them?" "Are my teammates relying on me for games?"

Practicing Does Not Replace Other Activities

Picking a time to practice is the same. Check your daily schedule for the best time of day to add another enjoyable activity. Just because you want to practice doesn't mean you have to give up or replace other interests. They are important too.

Happy Harry might enjoy practicing everyday in his English class. It might work out well for Harry, but what about the rest of the class? Find a time that is good for you, and that doesn't interrupt others or other activities.

Try to pick a specific time, for example, from 4:00 to 4:30 in the afternoon. Set it aside and stick to it. A specific time will allow you to concentrate only on practicing for that period. You can only give your attention to one thing at a time. When you've finished practicing, your mind is free to concentrate on your other interests and to fully enjoy them.

Caution: Don't Put It Off! Don't Procrastinate!

We all tend to put things off, but once we take the first step we enjoy plunging in. There are days when the hardest part about completing your homework is taking that first step, opening the book. There will also be days when the hardest part about practicing will be opening the instrument case, sitting at the piano bench, picking up that stick or pick or sounding a pitch on the pitch pipe.

The best advice is—Do It! When you finish your practice session the satisfaction will come not only from your musical progress, but also from the pride of overcoming procrastination, one of the major causes of inaction.

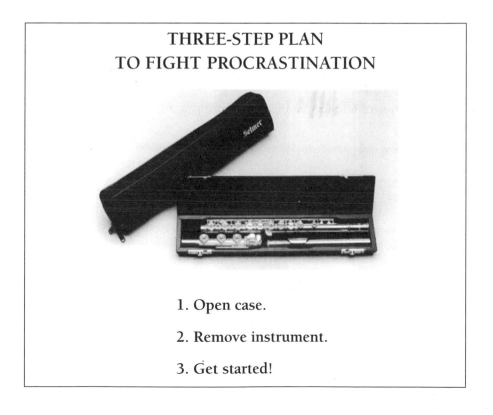

THREE-STEP PLAN TO FIGHT PROCRASTINATION

1. Open case.

2. Remove instrument.

3. Get started!

Where Should I Practice?

Picture yourself practicing in the middle of the school cafeteria during lunch. Although it sounds like fun, it would be hard to concentrate with all that noise and confusion.

There are times when parts of your home are just as busy and noisy! Avoid those places. Pick a place that is quiet so you can concentrate. If there's only one room that you can use, such as the room with the piano, discuss the time with your family. Ask them to leave that room available for your practice period. Again, a specific time set aside each day will make it easier for them to plan as well. By simply discussing these arrangements first, disagreements can be avoided.

Some Practice Rooms Are Better than Others

If, however, you have a choice of rooms, pick the one that gives you the best sound. Walk through each room and clap your hands, play your instrument or sing. Some rooms will give a soft sound while others will give a loud echo. A room that gives a soft sound makes your playing or singing sound muffled and weak. The sound from this type of room is sometimes referred to as a "dead sound." A room with too much echo gives a "live" or bouncy sound.

Try to find a room with a happy medium between these two extremes. If you pick a room with a "dead sound," you could get the impression that your tone is small and weak when that is not true. To compensate, it's easy to develop the bad habit of forcing the sound.

On the other hand, if the room is too "live," with too much echo, you could get the impression that your sound is bigger than it really is, and develop the bad habit of improper support.

Therefore, pick the room with a pleasing sound that is quiet enough so you can concentrate on what you want to accomplish.

Television Is Not a Good Practice Partner!

CAUTION! Don't pick a room where you can practice with the television on. You can only concentrate on one thing at a time. You can't concentrate on watching your favorite television show and practicing at the same time.

When you're practicing you're also developing your ears, listening to yourself and deciding what you like and what you want to improve. If your concentration is split between the television and practicing, developing good habits will be difficult.

What Materials Will I Need?

Did you ever sit down to write, have a great idea, reach for a pencil and by the time you found one, find that the idea had vanished, leaving you staring at a blank sheet of paper? The same thing can happen when you practice. Have all the materials you need ready. A sample check list might include your music, music stand, pencil, music manuscript paper, note paper, a mirror, metronome, tuner (see Chapter 6) and, especially, extras of breakable equipment like reeds, strings, guitar picks, drum sticks, etc.

Use a Music Stand

If your music is placed at the wrong height, you will be forced to bend over in order to see it. By doing so, you can develop bad habits regarding posture, breath control, hand position and other basics that lead to good musical development.

These potential problems can be avoided by simply using a music stand. Whether you practice sitting or standing, you can adjust a music stand to a comfortable height to assure proper breathing and physical contact with your instrument.

Don't Be Afraid to Use a Pencil

Why make the same mistake over and over when a little reminder will do the job? Don't be afraid to write in phrase marks, breath marks, bowings, problem sharps or flats, rhythm patterns, proper fingerings (especially alternate fingerings) and other musical thoughts.

Most of all, when questions arise, write them down before you forget them. Bring them to your teacher. The answers to general questions can save hours of wasted time, and can help you avoid developing bad habits.

Notes
Practice Planning

Part III

Methods of Practicing:
The Rewards of Good Planning

5

Planning Your Musical Agenda

Finally you've arrived! But, "How long will I stay?" "What will I see?" "What will I do in the amount of time I have?" Many of these questions, of course, were answered before you left on your trip. Now you can plunge in and enjoy the rewards of good planning.

Practicing also requires good planning. Before you plunge in you'll want to know, "How long will I stay?" and "What will I do in the amount of time I have?" How you practice, the methods you use, will be your musical agenda.

You're the Tour Guide

Your practice agenda will map out your musical travel, but as your own teacher, you're also the tour guide. Teachers know the interests of students. They plan class trips that will provide the most interesting ways for students to learn.

Being your own teacher is convenient and challenging. You decide what you want to accomplish and how best to accomplish it. You decide what your class -you- will be able to do better at the end of a practice session than you could at the start.

Below are methods to consider for planning your practice sessions.

Short Versus Long Practice Sessions

How long should each practice session be? That depends on your answers to two questions: "How long can I retain comfortable physical control of my instrument, or voice?" and "How long can I concentrate?" When comfortable physical control and concentration are lost, real practicing has stopped. Short practice sessions in which you retain both physical control and concentration are better than long practice sessions without them.

The amount of time spent is not as important as how it is spent. Practicing with a purpose will lead to progress and will avoid the development of bad habits.

Beginner's Math: 5 x 6 = 30 Is Better than 1 x 30 = 30

If you're a beginner you may want to practice a half hour (30 minutes) a day. But what if you can only control your instrument for five minutes? Does that mean you can't practice thirty minutes a day? Not at all. It does mean, however, that you'll get more from practicing if you practice five minutes six times a day. You'll feel fresh for each five minute session.

As your control and concentration increase, so can the length of your practice sessions. In a short time you can try practicing ten minutes three times a day, then fifteen minutes twice a day and finally, thirty minutes once a day. Gradually increasing your practice time is a healthy way to build muscles.

1 x 1 = 1 But 1 x 30 = 30

You can also leave your instrument out of its case, but in a safe place, and practice a technique or scale for a minute every time you pass it. All those minutes add up. They may also be a good change of pace from homework or other activities. One times thirty still equals thirty.

A Minute of Full Control Can Be a Long Time

Is a minute enough time to accomplish anything? Do a simple experiment and find out—it will only take a minute. Try doing continuous push-ups for one minute. That's approximately thirty push-ups. Did a minute seem shorter before the experiment?

Seconds Also Add Up

If you wanted to do thirty continuous push-ups, but you could only do one, should that stop you? It will only if you let it. If you can do one push-up, you will gain strength each time you do it. You could do your one push-up, and when that felt comfortable, try two, then three, then four and continue until you reach thirty.

MINUTE SCALE PRACTICE
How many times can you perform a scale in one minute?

Note value	Metronome mark	Number of times you can perform the scale in one minute
Half note	M.M. = 60	2
Half note	M.M. = 80	2.6
Half note	M.M. = 100	3.3
Half note	M.M. = 120	4
Quarter note	M.M. = 60	4
Quarter note	M.M. = 80	5.3
Quarter note	M.M. = 100	6.6
Quarter note	M.M. = 120	8
Eighth note	M.M. = 60	8
Eighth note	M.M. = 80	10.6
Eighth note	M.M. = 100	13.3
Eighth note	M.M. = 120	16

Is it worth a minute of your time?

You can do one fast push-up in one second! That's not much time, yet you'd be a little stronger from doing it. If you did one push-up thirty times throughout the day, by the end of the day you would have done thirty.

If you picked up your instrument thirty times and spent one minute improving skills, at the end of the day you would have practiced thirty minutes. Your muscles would be a little stronger, and you would increase your physical control. You would also avoid developing the bad habits that creep in when muscles get tired. When muscles get tired—rest them.

As you can see, the important word is consistency. Slow but steady still wins the race.

Can't Fool Me!

"Nice try, but you can't fool me," you might say. "My lesson materials aren't that hard. Why practice every day? I don't need it. My lesson is on Wednesday, so I can work on it the day before. I'll put all my time in at once. I'll practice one day a week and be done with it!"

That sounds logical. But if you practiced a half hour each of the six days before your lesson, you would have practiced 180 minutes (three hours).

Last Minute Preparation Doesn't Work

Try those push-ups again using the same logic. Your physical education homework is to do thirty push-ups a day, six days a week. That's 180 push-ups in six days. "My physical education test is on Wednesday. I just have to do 180 continuous push-ups the day before."

But when you try doing them you can only do ten. If you did all 180 the day before, instead of strengthening your muscles, you'd probably damage them. You'd have to wait for the muscles to heal, and then start over.

Whether practicing, doing push-ups or developing other skills, consistency with a purpose builds strength. With that strength comes confidence and the satisfaction of a job well done.

Studying Is No Different

Imagine Perfect Patricia and Backwards Bob studying for a spelling test. Patricia studied the spelling list five minutes at a time—only the amount of time she could concentrate. You guessed it, Bob was determined to study for an hour. Unfortunately, he couldn't concentrate after five minutes. For the remaining fifty-five minutes his mind wandered. He accidentally studied mis-spellings.

Had he stopped after five minutes, like Patricia, he would have eventually learned the correct spellings. Unfortunately, Bob studied misspellings ten times as long as he did the correct spellings. Now, like running the bases, he has to work twice as hard. First he must unlearn the misspellings before he can re-learn the correct ones. Bob might even quit.

Even if Bob and Patricia had concentrated as little as one minute at a time on the correct spelling of each word, they would have learned them eventually.

Listen to Yourself

The same is true of practicing. Let your muscles, mind and ears tell you how long each practice session should be. Practicing beyond your limits, like Bob's method of studying spelling, can sometimes do more harm than good.

Pace yourself at the beginning. Your practice sessions will rapidly get longer and more productive.

Practicing Slow Versus Practicing Fast

The Secret to Playing Fast Is Practicing Slow

What you can do slow, you can do fast with practice. What you think you can do fast, however, you may not be able to do slow. It sounds backwards, but it's true.

If you don't believe it, try those push-ups again. Do one push-up as fast as you can. Then, do one push-up as slow as you can. Which took more muscle control? Which gave you the feeling of muscles at work? Which made you more tired? Which challenged you to control your body? The slow push-up?

Try another experiment. Pick your most comfortable scale. Perform it as fast as you can. Then, perform it as slow as you can. Which method produced the best tone quality? Which had the best intonation (pitch relationships among scale tones)? Which one left you with the most pride and confidence in your performance? The slow one?

Practicing slow gives you time to listen and evaluate your performance. And, do it with confidence. Slow practice gives you time to concentrate on the musical as well as the technical. You can judge your performance by asking not only, "How fast can I manipulate this piece of machinery I call my instrument?" but, "How pleasant and musical are the sounds I'm producing?"

Practicing Fast By Practicing Slow

You can practice fast by practicing slow. Practicing slow gives you time to listen for, and develop, good tone quality and intonation, and accurate finger motion, as well as other qualities. As you gradually increase the speed, this good stuff goes along for the ride. It also gives you the opportunity to hear how different the same music sounds and feels at various tempos.

Wait a Minute!

"If I'm practicing slow," you might be thinking, "how can I learn to move my fingers fast?" True, playing fast takes precise motions. It also, however, takes confidence. The confidence gained from practicing slow also goes along for the ride as you gradually get faster.

Where Does Movement Take Place?

Compare examples A and B that follow. Which takes the fastest finger motion to move from one note to the other?

Example A   **Example B**

Things Aren't Always as They Seem

Logically, example B requires the fastest motion because a six-teenth note is faster than a whole note. That would be true if the change from one note to the next takes place on the note. Would you believe, however, that the motions are the same! The change from one note to the next doesn't take place on the note. The change takes place BETWEEN THE NOTES! Look at examples A and B again:

Example A   **Example B**

Notice the X between the notes in both examples. That's where the movement occurs. The first whole note in example A is held sixteen times longer than the first sixteenth note in example B before moving to the second note, and the second whole note in example A is held sixteen times longer after making the change than the second sixteenth note in example B. The movement between the notes, however, is the same. The only difference is how long the notes are held before and after the movement takes place.

As you go faster, you aren't moving quicker, but you are bringing the points of change closer together. Therefore, when you practice at a slow pace, using precise motions between notes, you're practicing fast by practicing slow.

Generally, start slow and gradually increase the speed. Don't get too fast too soon. You won't have time to listen. What you can't hear, you can't correct. What you don't correct, remains. Remember, anytime you do something repeatedly, you develop habits—good or bad.

Slow down, leave the bad habits on the roadside, and continue confidently.

Practicing Versus Playing

It's important to keep in mind that there is a difference between practicing and just playing.

Practicing Is Playing with a Purpose

You practice to improve technical skills and musicianship. Practicing is playing with a purpose. However, if you play through music, ignoring mistakes, or play pieces you can already play the way you have already played them, you won't improve.

It is also important to just play. Isn't that the reason you're practicing, to play music—to express yourself through sound? Of course it is. Playing, therefore, reinforces why you're practicing, but it shouldn't replace it.

Playing, however, is fun. It's a good way to reap the benefits of practicing and make music with friends. It's also a good way to review past lesson materials and play familiar music with ease. If you practice with a purpose, what you're practicing today will be what you'll be playing in the near future. That's progress!

Practicing Away from Your Instrument

At times you may become discouraged with practicing, and think, "I can't do that!" Don't get angry. It might be time to practice away from the instrument.

If practicing is getting you down, maybe it's because there's something you don't understand. Ask yourself: "Can I read the notes?" "Are there any symbols printed in the music that I don't know?" "Can I clap or sing the rhythm?" "Do I know the correct fingerings for all the notes?" "Can I sing what I want to play?" "Can I imagine the sounds that should be coming through my instrument or voice?" These questions lead to one main question, "Do I understand what I'm trying to do?"

Think It Through, then Try Again

If there is something that you don't understand, put the instrument down. Read the note names. Clap the rhythm patterns. Sing it. Then play or sing it again with a deeper understanding of the way it should sound. There will be times when practicing away from the instrument will accomplish more, in less time, than practicing with it.

Thinking through a problem will accomplish in a few minutes what mindless drilling may never accomplish.

Give Your Music Reading a Hand

Music notation is written on a staff. Regardless of what clef you read, the staff contains five lines and four spaces. Now, hold your hand out with your palm facing you. Surprise! Your four fingers and thumb supply the five lines of the staff, and the spaces between them supply the four spaces of the staff.

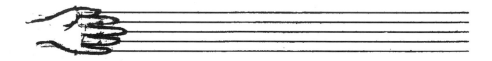

You can literally give your music reading a hand by using your hand to practice music reading. No matter where you are, it's handy to improve music reading skills.

Develop Your Ears: Put the Instrument Down

When you practice, you are your own teacher. At lessons, you rent your teacher's ears. Now, you must develop yours. Practicing away from your instrument is good ear training. You try to imagine the sound of what you see on the printed music. This will help develop your "inner hearing," your "musical ear"—a mental image of the printed page.

Give Those Muscles a Rest

Practicing away from the instrument also gives muscles a rest. When you continue, the muscles are relaxed and ready to go. Bad habits creep in when muscles get tired.

Control Your Thoughts and You Can Practice Anywhere

Developing the ability to practice without the instrument gives you the freedom to practice anywhere. If you can think, you can practice. You can practice on the school bus, in the library or while taking a walk. As long as you have control of your thoughts, you have control of your progress.

Practice on a Pencil

If you don't have an instrument, practice fingerings on a pencil. Sounds strange, but it works. Move your fingers on the pencil as you do on your instrument. You can feel if you're correct. You can also imagine the sound your instrument would make for each fingering—another good ear training exercise. Because a pencil has a flat surface, you will feel if fingers are not hitting the surface evenly. Best of all, a pencil doesn't make a sound, so you can practice on it anywhere.

Practicing Versus Studying

Practicing away from the instrument is another way of saying there's a difference between practicing and studying.

When you study a problem, you analyze it and make sure you understand what you're trying to do. After you have studied the problem, then practice it. Practicing helps develop the physical control necessary to perform what you've studied.

Successful practicing often depends on whether or not you've taken the time to study a problem before you attempt to do it. Ask yourself, "What do I need to understand about this piece before I can play or sing it?" and you've answered the question, "What can I practice away from the instrument?"

Remember, productive practicing takes place when you retain both physical control and concentration. Doesn't it make sense to separate them? Studying problem passages is an important part of practicing.

Knowing When to Stop

Some days, the hardest part about practicing is opening the case and getting started. To develop good habits, however, it's also important to know when to stop. After a period of time, your muscles will get tired and make it hard to concentrate. Why? Because you're human! Humans have limits. Don't get angry or frustrated. STOP! Some days, you feel better than others. You're not a machine that can be turned on and off. So, stop and come back later.

Building Good Relationships Takes Hard Work and Patience

Your instrument is a source of pleasure, but it may anger you at times. You may also become angry with your parents, brothers, sisters and friends, and solve the problem by removing yourself from the situation by leaving the room.

No matter how much you love someone or something, you can become angry with them. Your instrument is no different. When it angers and frustrates you, put it down—STOP. It may be the best way to retain a good relationship. If it happens too often, change where or how you practice. Most important, however, don't be afraid to discuss your concerns with your parents and teacher.

Remember, your instrument is your friend. Friends have occasional disagreements! Don't expect your relationship with your instrument to be perfect. Building good relationships takes hard work and patience!

6

Practice Methods in the Age of Technology

Practice Partners: Old Friends and New Acquaintances

Your basic practice partners will always be you, your instrument or voice and a clear image of what you want to accomplish.

Technology, however, supplies old and new practice partners. These practice partners, described below, can add other methods of practicing that can make your practice sessions more challenging and productive.

The Metronome: A Time Ticker

In four/four time, a quarter note gets one beat, a half note gets two beats and an eighth note gets half a beat. Notes longer than one beat, therefore, multiply the beat and notes shorter than one beat divide it. This assumes, however, that you know the length of the beat and that the beat remains steady. The metronome, an old and trusted practice partner, will help.

The first functional metronome was made in 1816 by Malzel. This is an important date to remember. It could affect the performance tempos you choose.

The metronome indicates the speed (tempo) of music by measuring the number of beats performed per minute. After 1816, composers could communicate the tempo they desired using this method.

Before the metronome, however, composers could only imply tempos. They used words, such as those listed below, to indicate how fast or slow their music should be performed. But, how fast is

---

COMMON TEMPO MARKS:
Words that Indicate Speed

Tempo mark	Definition
Largo	very slow, broad
Adagio	quite slow
Andante	at a walking pace
Moderato	moderate
Allegro	lively
Presto	very fast

fast? How slow is slow? Without the ability to measure movement, that was up to the performer.

Look at the definitions of the tempo marks again. Ask yourself, "Do all your friends walk (andante) at the same speed?" "If they're running to the bus *presto,* do some run faster than others?" You can see how inexact these terms can be. The metronome changed that. It lets you walk and run at the same pace.

A metronome has printed numbers, ranging from low to high, that indicate the number of beats per minute. If you set the metronome to 60, for example, there will be 60 beats per minute. If you set the metronome to 120, there will be 120 beats per minute— twice as fast. Therefore, the lower the number, the slower the tempo, the higher the number, the faster the tempo. By starting on a low number and gradually going higher, you're increasing the speed.

Below are pictures of two metronomes. The pendulum model was the original type of construction used by Malzel. Today, however, most metronomes are digital, smaller and more accurate. All

Pendulum Metronome

Digital Metronome

metronomes, however, will "tick" at the number of beats per minute to which they are set.

Metronomes are excellent partners for practicing fast by practicing slow (Chapter 5). They help you retain a steady tempo, develop rhythmic accuracy, become sensitive to tempo changes, develop even finger, tongue, bow, pick or stick motion, or simply give you the exact tempo indicated on the music. The metronome marking, M.M. = plus a number, is located on the left side of the sheet music above the first staff, as illustrated below.

SOLDIER'S MARCH

The Tuner:
============

The Tuner: Don't Be a Fish Out of Water

You can't tune-a-fish, but you must tune your instrument. A fish has scales that can't be tuned, instruments have scales that must be tuned. Musicians who don't listen carefully to tune the scales on their instruments are like fish out of water—especially when playing with other musicians.

No instrument (with the exception of some electronic instruments), regardless of its quality, is perfectly in tune with itself. It's the player's responsibility to listen and to make minute pitch adjustments.

Just as the metronome is a great practice partner for developing rhythmic skills, the tuner is a great practice partner for developing accurate intonation and good tone quality. As mentioned before, if you try to concentrate on all the little things that go into producing a musical sound, you can drive yourself crazy. If, however, you produce both accurate intonation and good tone quality, you're probably doing all the little things correctly.

How Does It Work?

Tuners measure pitch levels. Most modern tuners are digital, and indicate pitch levels by numbers above and below "0," as shown in the picture below.

The "0" indicates the desired pitch level. The numbers to the right of the "0" indicate that the pitch is above the desired level, and the numbers to the left of the "0" indicate that the pitch is below the desired level.

When you play or sing a tone, the tuner measures its vibrations. The indicator, usually a needle, shows if you are at the desired pitch level, above the desired pitch level (sharp) or below the desired pitch level (flat).

There are many uses for tuners depending on the instrument you play, the voice part you sing, your stage of development and what skills you're trying to improve. A tuner will help you become more sensitive to pitch so that you will gain insight into the pitch adjustments necessary on your instrument.

Ask to borrow your teacher's tuner and give it a try.

Modern Stereo

One hundred years ago people heard music performed live or they didn't hear it at all.

Today, with modern stereo equipment, you can listen to any type of music and hear it with a quality of sound that rivals a live performance. You can listen to music at home, in the car or anywhere you like. In fact, it's difficult to go shopping, ride an elevator or go to a restaurant without hearing music.

FM Radio Is a Good Teacher

Your home or car FM radio is a good practice partner for hearing musical styles. Radios can be pre-set to stations of your choosing so you can quickly switch from one station to another. If, for example, you program your radio's pre-sets to a classical music station, a jazz station, a rock station, or a country station, you can explore a variety of musical styles. By listening to each station, you'll become familiar with these musical styles.

You might also find that you enjoy listening to more than one type of music. It can be an enriching experience as you learn to listen to and appreciate new styles of music. Tastes change and grow; you may even be surprised at yourself.

What Does this Have to Do with Practicing?

In order to perform various styles of music, it's necessary to know what each sounds like. Hearing a wide range of musical styles will be helpful in interpreting music. Listening gives you both a model for the music you're practicing and a reason to practice it.

Play Along

Background accompaniments on cassettes and CDs are available in all musical styles to use on your home stereo. You practice the music, then put on the accompaniment, and have a ball playing or singing along. The tempos of these accompaniments, however, can't be altered. Computers, on the other hand, allow you to change tempos, and will be discussed in the next section.

Hi-Tech Practice Partners

In the past, practice tools were simple: your instrument, method book, a music stand, maybe a metronome and a pencil.

Times change. Technology has added many new tools and new uses for old ones. Now television is used for videos and interactive video games, as well as being part of a multimedia home entertainment system.

Computers, which your parents may not have had when they were your age, help you learn almost any aspect of any subject, including music.

Music technology opens new doors and adds new methods of learning. This section introduces some categories of music technology that can make practicing more exciting than it was not too many years ago.

Only categories of technology, not brand names, will be mentioned. Technology is constantly changing, and new products are being introduced. However, the general categories will most likely remain constant. You'll have to check to be sure that the software you choose is compatible with your computer and that it meets your musical needs.

New Uses for Television: Videos Contain More than Movies

There are videos on every topic imaginable. Make use of them. You can see performances of all musical styles and watch the musicians as you listen. Videos can also help you learn about any aspect of music, including music theory and music history. These subjects will give you a better understanding of the music you're practicing.

"How To" videos are also available. Videos are available that cover every aspect of musical performance, from making your own oboe reeds to playing heavy metal guitar. Check catalogs, or ask your teachers for suggestions.

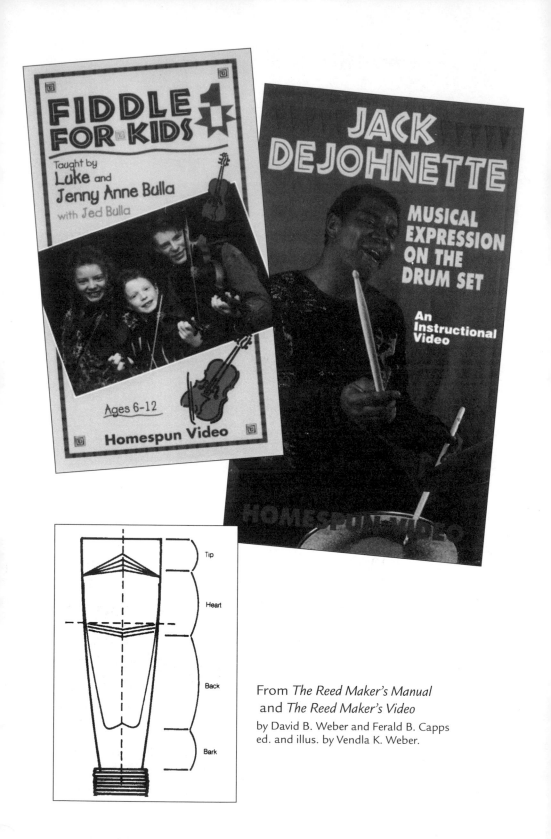

From *The Reed Maker's Manual*
and *The Reed Maker's Video*
by David B. Weber and Ferald B. Capps
ed. and illus. by Vendla K. Weber.

From *Finding Your Way with Hand Drums* (John Bergamo)—Interworld Music

Personal Computers

No matter what brand of home computer your family has, there's software to help you learn more about music. Much of this software is interactive, making it fun to learn more about the music you're practicing and the composers who wrote it. You'll find software that will meet your needs and interests at all levels of difficulty.

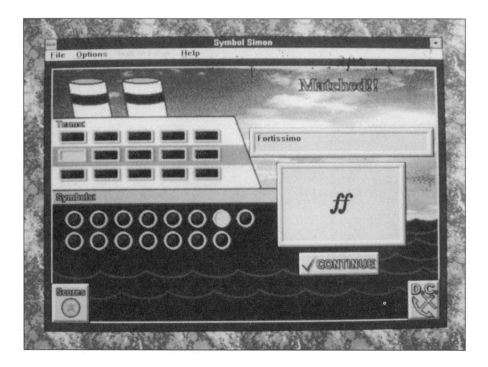

Computers Make Wonderful Practice Partners

What about practicing with the computer? Computers are wonderful practice partners. Whether you program your own accompaniments or use pre-programmed midi files, you can play along with

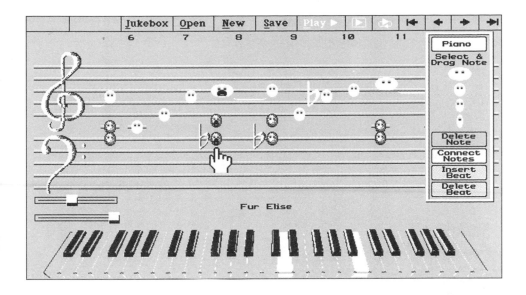

the computer. Do you like to play classical music, jazz, rock, or country, or do you prefer to improvise? Software is available that lets you play or sing in any style, in any key and at any tempo with just a few clicks of the mouse.

Choose the Tempo and the Key

Computers are digital. They store numbers, 1's and 0's, that are converted into sounds. Because the computer processes numbers and not sound waves, you can choose the tempo and the key. With accompaniments that are frozen in one tempo and key, like the pre-recorded accompaniments for home stereo use, this isn't possible.

Practice with a Symphony or a Rock Band

Add a synthesizer, module or sound card to your computer and you can have your accompaniments played by any instrument or combination of instruments you like. You can practice any musical style with the appropriate instruments.

Synthesizer

Sound Module/Tone Generator

Why Not Compose and Practice Your Own Music?

With computer software, you can enter your own compositions, and experiment with your original musical ideas. You don't always have to perform music written by someone else. With most music software you can print out your compositions as sheet music and play them with friends.

If you have a computer, only your imagination sets the limits for its use.

CD ROMs

CD ROMs, like computer software, offer a variety of topics and uses that can enhance practicing. Again, check catalogs and check with your teachers. New materials are constantly being released. Make good use of them.

Music Technology Can Be a Two-Way Street

Music technology enhances your practicing, but it doesn't replace the reason for practicing. Properly used, music technology can be a two-way street. It will help you accomplish more during your practice sessions, and it will help you learn more about what you're practicing.

Today, computer skills play an important role in all your school subjects and areas of interest. Let your interest in music technology help you increase your general computer skills, or let your developed computer skills introduce you to music technology. It's a two-way street that's worth traveling.

Notes

Methods of Practicing

Part IV

The Arrival:
Your Destination

7

It's Time to
Play the Game

You've come a long way. You mapped your trip in Part II, discovered various methods of transportation in Part III and now you've arrived.

Of all the possible places you could have visited, you know WHY you chose the one you did. The fun you'll have now depends on WHAT you do during your stay.

If you visited a city that was the home of a major league team during the baseball season, seeing your favorite team might be on the agenda. You'd probably get to the stadium early to see the teams warm up and play the game.

WHY watch warm-up practice, the game's WHAT you came to see? Warm-up practice isn't the game. Or is it?

Understand "Why", then Supply "What"

Why play baseball? To enjoy playing the game! Then what skills does a player need? To play baseball, a player needs the ability to hit, catch and throw the ball, run bases, and understand the rules of the game. By understanding the rules of the game, a player knows when each skill is used in a game situation. By knowing "why" each skill is needed, a player knows "what" to practice.

Playing an instrument and playing baseball have much in common. Why play an instrument? To enjoy playing music! Then, what are the *skills* you'll need to be a musician?

Where baseball players practice daily to sharpen skills in hitting, catching, throwing and running, musicians practice daily to sharpen skills in tone quality, intonation, breath control, finger control, articulation, dynamics, interpretation and sight-reading.

Musicians and baseball players would get bored if they practiced but never played the game. However, by understanding "why" the skills are needed, they know "what" to practice. A baseball team's pre-game practice warm-ups may not be part of the game, but they determine how successfully the game is played.

Understanding "why" and then supplying "what" gives practicing a purpose.

The Game of Music: Understanding "Why"

Play Ball! The game's beginning. People are shouting and jumping out of their seats. You can't understand a word they're saying, but you know how they feel—you share in the excitement.

That's the game of music! Feelings! Expressing emotions through sound. Communicating through sound what words can't express.

Music is another language, only its vocabulary is organized sound. Practicing is studying music's vocabulary. In a sense, you're studying music as a second language.

How often have you thought, "I know how I feel, but I can't find the right words to express it!" You're not alone. People have had the same problem for centuries. They often solved it through music and the visual arts. They developed languages for expressing emotions. It's been going on since the cavemen painted pictures of animals on cave walls.

History is fascinating. History books, however, can only explain where people lived, how they lived, and what they did. Their music and arts, however, are our only link to the way they felt.

Sharing feelings, past and present, is the game of music.

Game Equipment:
One Time Machine

To play baseball you need a bat, ball and glove. To play music you need a time machine—your instrument. With your instrument you become an explorer. You can transport yourself back to any time in history and then return to the present by just turning a page.

The Rules of the Game:
Being Musical

Practicing will develop the skills to control that time machine, but the results can be mechanical. Your instrument consists of more than keys, strings, bows, picks, sticks or vocal chords. The most important part of it is you. Without you, the instrument is worthless.

By adding you, your feelings, you change the mechanical to the musical.

Being musical supplies the rules of the game. The game will never get dull because the rules change from day to day, as you change from day to day.

Exploring emotions, past and present, yours and others—that's being musical. That's being human. That's playing the game of music!

You Supply "What"

You've decided that visiting the past and having a better understanding of the present is worth the effort. But what about the future, that's where the real adventure is—the unknown.

If you could travel five years into the future, what kind of musician would you like to be? Obviously, you can't do today what you'd like to be able to do in five years, but you can start your trip.

Like you, your musical skills grow day to day. With your teacher's help, each week can bring you closer to where you want to be. That weekly travel consists of your daily practice sessions, practice sessions designed to build a balance of skills needed to play the game.

The game of music is also referred to as interpretation—making the music sound the way you think it should. All the skills you develop, tone quality, intonation, dynamics, finger control and articulation, must be at your fingertips when the game calls for them. They're the "what" that you supply.

8

Developing a Balanced Technique:
Planning Daily Practice Sessions

You're ready to roll up your sleeves and get in the game. You know why you're playing, and what techniques you'll have to practice. Before you charge out on the playing field, however, keep in mind that the skills (technique) you develop must be balanced. You can't be successful if you can throw the ball, but you can't catch it.

Unfortunately, many young musicians think that technique means "How fast can I play?" Developing speed is one area of technique, but without building a balance of skills, speed may never come. (Review "Practicing Fast by Practicing Slow," Chapter 5).

Beware, it's also easy to fall into the time trap, and think, "Gee, I practiced a half hour. I'm bushed—what a workout!" Stop, ask yourself, "What could I do at the end of the half hour that I couldn't do at the beginning?" Your answer will tell you the value of the time spent. Unless you start with a purpose, you can't end with a sense of satisfaction.

Ice Cream without Spinach Won't Build Muscles

Think about that chocolate cake again. If your imagination gets carried away, add a scoop of ice cream.

Wouldn't it be great to have ice cream as your main course three meals a day? Imagine the fun you'd have planning a menu of your favorite flavors. It wouldn't be long, however, before you heard a voice saying, "Ice cream alone isn't a balanced diet! You have to eat foods from all four food groups. Ice cream's fine, but ice cream without spinach won't build muscles!"

Practicing is your musical meal time, and it also has its ice cream. You may enjoy ice cream more than spinach, and you may enjoy playing songs more than practicing scales. Why not enjoy both, one as part of the main course, and the other for dessert? Balanced practice builds musical muscles.

Planning Balanced Practice Sessions

Looking back at the list of technical skills, on page 84, you might be wondering, "How can I practice each technical area daily and still have time for my lesson material?"

Divide and Conquer

One answer comes from the way you divide your practice time. For example, if you plan to practice one half hour, and spend approximately five minutes on warm-ups, seven minutes on scales and exercises, fifteen minutes applying skills to pieces you're working on and three minutes sight-reading, your practice time will be balanced and more interesting.

This is, of course, only one example. Time proportions will change from day to day or week to week, but with your teacher's help, you can plan practice sessions that are right for you.

Warm-Up to Limber Up

The warm-up segment of your practice session supplies you with another answer to your question. Unfortunately, many students don't include them. Warm-ups offer brief but consistent opportunities to practice all areas of a balanced technique. Warm-ups are focused mini-practice sessions within your practice time. Warm-ups let you concentrate on one particular skill at a time.

Warm-ups also limber up your mind and body with healthy

stretching exercises that help you approach the main portion of your practicing with well-tuned skills.

The pre-game warm-up you saw at the baseball game does the same for athletes. Their warm-ups prepare them physically and mentally to meet the demands of the game. Without warming up, they would injure the muscles they rely on, and they wouldn't have the concentration needed for the game.

Practicing is no different. Warm-ups get you physically and mentally prepared to give your best to your practice session. They're as important to musicians as they are to athletes.

The Five-Minute-a-Day Exercise Plan for Balanced Warm-Ups

The remainder of this chapter describes the areas of a balanced technique. If your warm-up includes as little as one minute a day on each area, you'll develop technical control and musicianship simultaneously. Best of all, you'll do it in as little as five minutes a day.

The important word is consistency. Like the one-second push-up, a minute of concentrated effort on each area of technique will make you a little stronger for having done it.

Building Musical Muscles: A Balanced Technique

Good tone quality and intonation supply the foundation for a balanced technique. It's impossible to concentrate on every aspect of technique at the same time, yet if you're satisfied with your tone quality and intonation, you're probably doing the little things correctly.

A Beautiful Tone Needs Your Support

It takes a strong support system for a beautiful tone quality with good intonation. We can't see the support. We take it for granted. But it's there.

Give Your Tone Quality and Intonation a Lift

Have you ever watched a mechanic repair a car? The car's put on a hydraulic lift. What do you watch? Your concentration is probably on the car suspended in air. You forget that there's a strong force supporting it. To get a beautiful tone quality, you're the support system—the foundation, the hydraulic lift that supports it.

The type of support system depends on your instrument's sound source, how the sound is set into motion. Whether it's the air stream, a bow drawn across a string, a pick, a finger or a stick— it becomes the foundation of your tone. How you control the source will determine the tone quality you get.

Ask your teacher for warm-up exercises that will strengthen control of your instrument's sound source. These exercises will supply a firm foundation for developing all other skills. Now let's look at the areas of a balanced technique: tone quality, intonation, finger control, articulation and dynamics, and see what each has to offer your musical development.

Tone Quality

Tone quality is the unique sound of each instrument. It's the voice an instrument uses to communicate. That's why you can listen to music and say, "Hey, listen to that trumpet—I like the sound of brass instruments," "The oboe sounded haunting there," "Is that a soprano or alto saxophone? Is that a violin or a viola? I think that's a string patch on the synthesizer!" You attached names to familiar sounds, just as you attach names and faces to familiar voices.

You can identify instruments because, like you, they belong to families. Each family shares methods of producing the vibrations that set sound into motion. These are the sound sources, referred to above, that control tone quality.

That doesn't mean, however, that you'll sound exactly like everyone else who plays the same instrument. How often have you heard performers, and identified the performer and the instrument? You can identify both because performers develop tone qualities that are as unique as their speaking voices. You can do the same. Your tone quality makes you an individual. It gives you a musical voice.

Introduce Yourself and Listen

Your voice is often another person's first contact with you. Musically, your tone quality is the listener's first contact with you. Like your speaking voice, your tone quality can be pleasant, harsh or dull. The more control you have of your speaking voice, the easier it is to express your feelings. Musically, the same is true of your tone quality.

To improve tone quality—listen. Listen to music performed on your instrument. Listen to yourself. Create an image of what a good tone quality is, and match it.

Listen to all styles of music. Tone quality that's appropriate for one style may not be appropriate for another. The more you listen, the easier it is to decide what kind of tone quality you like, what kind you don't like and how you want your musical voice to sound.

Hold It!

Controlling your instrument's sound source takes strength. Strength is built through slow and consistent exercise: holding long tones, practicing slow scales (rudiments for percussionists) or pieces that require sustained tones. These will also help develop flexibility—control of the full range of your instrument. (See Chapter 5, "Practicing Fast by Practicing Slow.")

With all that a good tone quality can do for you, isn't it worth the effort? Good tone quality will supply the foundation for the other areas of a balanced technique, just as a cement foundation supplies the support for a house.

Intonation

The car you saw being repaired might have needed a tune-up. Machines run rough and sound out of tune if all parts aren't working correctly. Your instrument, a musical machine, will only sound smooth if it's in tune.

Intonation is playing or singing at correct pitch levels, commonly referred to as "being in tune." Most instruments are not perfectly in tune, and minor pitch adjustments must be made as you play them. Therefore, you are the mechanic and your ears are your tool kit.

You judge if you're in tune, at the proper pitch level, or out of tune, "sharp" or "flat." If the pitch is "sharp," it will be above the desired pitch level. If it's "flat," it will be below the desired pitch level. Correct fingerings alone will not ensure that notes are "in tune."

Use Your Practice Room Upstairs

Listen carefully to the pitch levels of individual tones and the pitch relationships between tones. Use your practice room upstairs—your mental image of the pitches. Imagine the sounds, then play them. Sing them! When you practice scales and intervals, listen for the distances between the tones and become accustomed to their sounds. If you can imagine and sing them, you will make the necessary adjustments without realizing it.

Tone quality and intonation work as a team. Remember, you can't tune-a-fish, but you must tune your instrument. Don't be a fish out of water. (See Tuner, Chapter 6.)

Finger Control

Finger Control and Scales Go Hand in Hand

If your instrument has keys or strings, your fingers will control them. Finger control means developing proper contact with the keyboard of your instrument. Finger control and scales go hand in hand. Together they will help develop technique and musicianship.

Scales: Your "Keys to Success"

Happy Harry might even say that scales are your "KEYS TO SUCCESS!" And a wonderful key ring it is. There are two types of scales—major and minor. Both, however, can be built above each of the twelve half steps of the octave. By doing simple math, 2 x 12, you can see that musicians have twenty-four versions of the two scales as their basic vocabulary.

Scales and the Musical Triangle

From 1600, the Baroque Period of music history, to the present, most Western music has been based on major and minor scales. Composers use scales to write music, and listeners expect to hear them in most musical styles.

That leaves you, the interpreter, to complete the musical triangle. You practice scales to develop the skills to perform the works of composers for your listeners. The more comfortable you feel with scales, the easier it will be to perform any style of music.

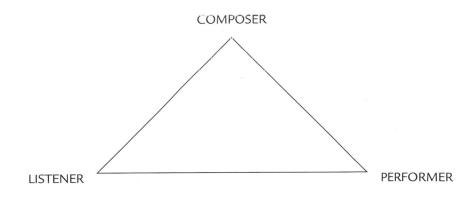

COMPOSER

LISTENER   PERFORMER

Practicing Scales: There's Good News and Bad News

Let's get the bad news out of the way first. The bad news is that it's difficult to perform music without practicing scales. But is that bad news or a fallacy?

Unfortunately, many young musicians put practicing scales in the same category as going to the dentist or studying for a test. They think that their parents make them practice scales as a punishment for not cleaning their room, and that their teachers make them practice scales as a punishment for not practicing.

They're wrong! They don't recognize the value of scale study. They don't realize that scales aren't a punishment. They don't realize that scales are more than exercises. Most of all, they don't realize that scales are a gift.

Good News: One Key Can Open Millions of Doors!

Now the good news! Scales are the keys to opening countless numbers of musical doors—old doors to past centuries of Western music and new doors to most of today's music.

By practicing major and minor scales, you're practicing all the written music that's based on them. You could be practicing millions of pieces at the same time. That sounds a little too good to be true, but it is.

When you practice the C major scale, for example, you're practicing all the music that was ever written in the key of C major—whether it's Beethoven's First Symphony in C Major, Mozart's "Jupiter" Symphony in C Major or the latest popular song.

When the title of a piece includes C major, as in Beethoven's

Symphony #1 in C Major, it simply means that the composition is based on the C major scale. If it's based on the C major scale, it's in the key of C. The same is true for other pieces and other scales. By practicing scales you're practicing most of the music that has already been written, as well as music that will be written in the future.

Look at all you can accomplish by practicing scales. The sooner you start, the sooner the world of Western Music will open to you.

C Major Scale—Treble Clef

Ode to Joy

Treble clef

Beethoven

C Major Scale—Bass Clef

Ode to Joy

Bass clef

Beethoven

C Major Scale—Alto Clef

Ode to Joy

Alto clef

Beethoven

When Practicing Scales, You Can't Fool Mother Nature: Start Slow!

As a young child, you learned to crawl, then walk and then run. You couldn't run before you crawled because you had to go through one stage to develop the next. In short, you couldn't fool Mother Nature.

When practicing scales or other skills, follow Mother Nature's model. Start slow and gradually increase the speed to develop strength and control. You may feel like your fingers are crawling, but when they run up and down the keyboard, they'll do it with confidence.

Use scales to practice fast by practicing slow. You'll gain finger control plus improve tone quality and intonation at the same time. Why lose good tone quality and intonation just to see how fast you can play? (See Practicing Fast by Practicing Slow, Chapter 5 and The Metronome, Chapter 6.)

Again, follow Mother Nature's Musical Law of Development: Practice exercises, whether they're scales, studies or difficult passages, from slow to fast. As you gradually increase the speed, you'll retain all the good stuff: tone quality, intonation and confidence.

Remember, what you can do slow you can do fast with practice, but what you THINK you can do fast you may not be able to do when you slow down and listen carefully.

Practice Scales with Musical Thought: Phrase Them!

A phrase is a complete musical thought. As in written and spoken language, a musical thought either pauses, like a comma, or ends, like a period. Practice slow scales to get the feeling of the musical phrase. Each phrase has a beginning, a middle and an end. So does a scale. The top of the ascending scale and the bottom of the descending scale are the periods, and the halfway points are the commas, as shown in the following examples.

C Major Scale with Phrase Marks—Treble Clef

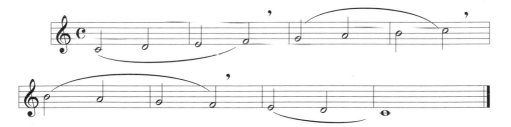

C Major Scale with Phrase Marks—Bass Clef

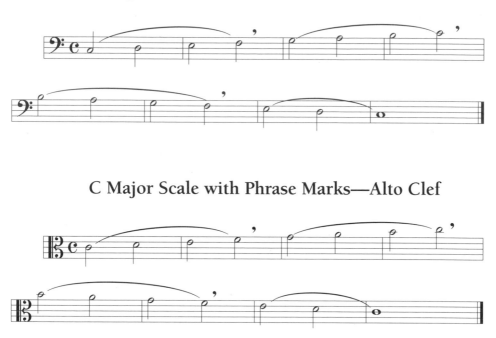

C Major Scale with Phrase Marks—Alto Clef

Classical Music and All that Jazz and Rock

Look through the pieces you're practicing and find all the passages that are scales or sections of scales. You'll be surprised at how many you'll find. If you've practiced scales, you've practiced parts of these pieces before. It's easier to play what you've already practiced many times.

That's true of classical music, but what about popular music? As mentioned earlier, popular music uses the same notes, skills and scales as classical music. The difference is the musical style. When you listen to popular music you may hear performers improvising—composing as they play or sing. You can develop these skills with the scales you've practiced.

There are many unfamiliar terms in the study of popular music—Dorian Mode, Phyrgian Mode, chord changes, among others. Believe it or not, every time you practice scales, like those in the following examples, you're practicing what jazz and rock musicians use as the basis for their improvised solos.

C Major Scale by Step—Treble Clef

C Major Scale by Step—Bass Clef

C Major Scale by Step—Alto Clef

Look at the same example below. Notice that each step of the scale, as it is used in classical music, can be used differently in popular music for improvisation. You've already practiced the modes you may read about. It's just a matter of realizing that they have other uses. By thinking of them in another way, you're practicing classical and popular music at the same time.

C Major Scale by Step—Mode Names Added

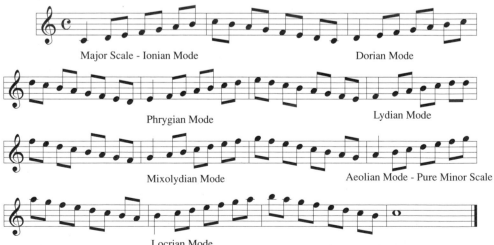

It's always essential to remember that THE WAY YOU THINK IS THE WAY YOU PLAY. And the way you think about the materials you practice will determine what you get from them. As your musical interests expand, you'll have the skills to grow with them.

So What's the Point?

Whether you eventually use your skills for classical music, jazz, rock, country, gospel, new age or any other style, the techniques you practice are the same. Why not add one more element to your practice session. Thinking! Thinking of the various ways you can enjoy using the materials you're practicing.

Articulation: Speaking Musically

To Say What You Mean, Articulate Clearly

"School's canceled today." Read it out loud. Repeat it as a question. Read it again. Sound disappointed. Sound excited! Notice that the same words can have different meanings depending on your inflection and verbal punctuation. If you wrote that sentence, your meaning would change with the punctuation mark you chose.

Words are to spoken language what notes are to music. Articulation marks in music indicate the various ways that notes can be pronounced. Composers use articulation marks to add meaning to notes, as writers use punctuation marks to add meaning to words. Both require clear articulation to be understood and to be effective.

Good Tone Quality Is the Foundation of Clear Articulation

Clear articulation depends on an even, sustained sound. Whether the sound is set into motion by the air stream, a bow, a stick, a pick or fingers, the sustained tone will supply the firm foundation.

Slow practice, used to develop tone quality and intonation, will provide that foundation for control of articulation. Clear articulation is the sustained tone sliced into measured lengths.

Slicing the Bologna

The sustained sound is like a long rolled bologna at the grocery deli counter. When you articulate notes, you're slicing that bologna into desired lengths.

Each family of instruments has a unique method of setting the sound into motion. That method determines how the bologna is sliced, and the flavor it has. That's no bologna! All musicians gain communication skills by developing clear articulation.

Generally, articulation studies help wind players coordinate movement of the breath, tongue and fingers—string players (including the guitar family), coordinate the finger movement of the left hand with the bow, pick or fingers of the right hand—keyboard players, control variations in finger attack and pressure—percussionists, control sticks and wrists and singers, coordinate breath and tongue.

Four Ways to Slice the Bologna

Composers use four basic articulation marks to indicate how they want notes attacked (pronounced):

- –   **Legato** (–), a smooth attack giving the note its full value.
- .   **Staccato** (.), a crisp attack making the notes shorter (approximately half the printed value).
- >   **Accent** (>), adding extra emphasis to the beginning of the note.
- sfz   **Sforzando** (sfz), an explosive attack.

In each of the examples below, the whole notes are the rolls of bologna and the quarter notes are the slices. Try them—taste the difference.

A Smooth Sandwich Slice—Slicing the Bologna Legato Style

Bologna Tid-Bits—Slicing the Bologna Staccato Style

Chew Harder on the Down Bite—Slicing the Bologna Accent Style

Enjoy the Explosive Flavor—Slicing the Bologna Sforzando Style

Musically speaking, clear articulations provide the clarity needed to speak musically.

Dynamics

To Be Dynamic, Use Dynamics

"Lower your voice, don't yell!" "Please speak up, I can't hear you." How many times have you heard comments like those referring to how loud or soft you speak?

When you're excited because you got an A on a test, or when you hit a home run, does your voice reflect your excitement? Your ability to express feelings depends on your ability to vary the volume levels of your voice. That adds a dynamic quality to what you are saying.

Dynamics refer to how soft or loud you play or sing. Musically, your instrument is your voice, and your ability to express yourself depends on your ability to vary your voice's volume levels.

Dynamics Are Relative

Dynamics are relative. Like brothers, sisters or cousins, they're members of the same family—a family of symbols that indicate degrees of loud and soft.

How loud is loud and how soft is soft? Think of someone talking in a library at normal voice level when everything else is quiet. That normal voice suddenly sounds very loud. If the same person spoke in the same normal voice while watching a 100-yard run at a football game, however, you wouldn't be able to hear it. How loud is loud? It's relative. It depends on where you are and what you're doing.

Dynamics are relative to the instrument you play. Each instrument has its own dynamic range. A flute can't play as loud as a tuba, and a piano can't play as loud as a church organ.

Dynamics are relative as well to the style of music and the historical period in which a piece of music was written. A string quartet doesn't perform with the same dynamic range as a brass quartet, and a concert band or symphony orchestra can't play as loud as a fully amplified rock band.

Listening to all styles of music will help you become sensitive to the dynamic level appropriate for each.

Mezzo Forte: Sit Right in the Middle

The most important thing to remember, however, is that dynamics are relative to each other. Although there is no exact definition of how loud is loud and how soft is soft, there are six standard notation symbols that indicate gradations of volume from soft to loud. These symbols are:

pianissimo (pp)   very soft

piano (p)   soft

mezzo piano (mp)   moderately soft

mezzo forte (mf)   *moderately loud*

forte (f)   loud

fortissimo (ff)   very loud

Mezzo forte sits in the middle, half way between piano (p) and fortissimo (ff).

Practicing Dynamics

Mezzo forte is your comfortable, normal playing or singing dynamic. It's also the guide for judging the others. Keep in mind, however, that regardless of how loud or how soft you get, you must always be in full control of your instrument or voice.

Dynamics, Tone Quality, and Intonation Are Teammates

Dynamics, tone quality and intonation are often practiced together. As you change from loud to soft or from soft to loud be careful to retain good tone quality and intonation.

Generally, practicing dynamics consists of working on control of a sustained dynamic level, as shown in example A, or controlling the gradual changes from one dynamic level to another, crescendo (getting gradually louder) and diminuendo (getting gradually softer), as shown in example B. Dynamics make wonderful additions to daily warm-up exercises.

Example A   Example B

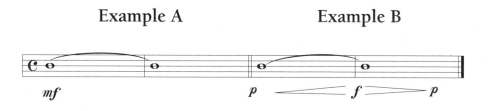

Remember, to be dynamic, use dynamics!

9

Putting It All Together:

A Balanced Technique Goes to Work

Developing a balanced technique takes focused and consistent practice. But, when you're interpreting and sight-reading music, you'll find it was worth the effort. Now, let's put that technique to work.

Interpretation: Be Yourself!

When interpreting music—you're the boss. You're presenting your musical personality to listeners. All the technical skills you've practiced are the tools for interpreting music.

Interpretation is the game of music, making the music sound the way you want it to. It's changing your mental image into sound. It's your musical destination, where you enjoy the rewards of practicing.

You'll also reap the rewards of listening when you begin interpreting music. By listening to music, you've built a vocabulary of mental images of musical styles. When applied, this vocabulary will supply added tools for interpreting music and reference points for developing your own musical ideas.

Music history and music theory are other valuable tools to help you make musical decisions. The more you know about the music you're performing, the more you'll appreciate it, and the easier it will be to make your interpretation stylistically correct. (See Practice Partners, Chapter 6.)

Improvisation: Be the Composer and Interpreter at the Same Time

Interpretation doesn't only refer to printed music. It can also refer to music created through improvisation, or composing as you perform. Improvisation is usually associated with jazz and popular music. Improvisation, however, has a long history and is part of many musical styles. It's great fun to challenge yourself to create your own music and develop a personal musical style.

The computer and home stereo are good practice partners for experimenting with musical ideas. They'll help add new excitement to old exercises. (See Practice Partners, Chapter 6.)

Relax: Take It Easy and Be Creative

Our best ideas sometimes slip in when we relax. How many times has an idea popped out of nowhere while you were sitting under a tree, taking a walk or a shower? That's no surprise—after working at something for a long time our minds can get tired. Then, when we relax, poof! Everything suddenly seems clear as a bell!

Relax, and come back refreshed! At times, you can accomplish more by freeing your mind and letting it do its job. (See Practicing Away from the Instrument and Knowing When to Stop, Chapter 5.)

Countless Possibilities: Pick One!

When you're interpreting music, you have musical decisions to make. Any piece of music, however, can have countless interpretations. How do you pick one?

One way is to sing. Singing is natural, you just do it. You don't have to worry about music reading and technical concerns. You sing and enjoy the music. If you like, you can sing the same piece a hundred different ways before deciding which one you like best.

Singing is one of the best ways to get musical ideas. After you sing, transfer what you sang to your instrument. In this way, you're combining the technical skills you've developed through practicing exercises with the mental, or musical, skills you've developed through listening and singing. Good musicians play the way they sing.

If you have a problem interpreting a piece of music, take a walk, ride your bike, sing for a mile or so, and come back physically and musically fit!

Sight-Reading

The More You Read, the Faster You Read

How long would it take to read one page if you had to stop, sound out each word and then look it up in a dictionary? The more you read, however, the more your reading skills improve. Soon it only takes a few minutes to read a page the first time. You read faster and with greater comprehension.

Declare Your Musical Independence

The same applies to reading music. Sight-reading is the ability to look at a new piece of music and play it or sing it the first time— on sight. If you've ever said, "How does it go?—If I know how it goes, I can play it," then sight-reading is for you. You need to become musically independent. Sight-reading will provide that independence. And, with musical independence, comes the freedom to explore new music on your own.

Invest a Few Minutes Now and Save Hours in the Future

You have a new piece of music. It's one page long, and will take two minutes to perform after you've practiced it. But, how long will it take to practice it? Depending on your skills and the difficulty of the piece, you might say a day, a week, a month. But how long would it take if you could play it the first time? Two minutes! What a difference! That's what sight-reading can do for you. It's worth the effort.

Why waste time? A few minutes a day now improving sight-reading will save hours in the future.

To Improve Sight-Reading, Sight-Read!

There's only one way to improve sight-reading. Sight-read! Do it consistently and your skills will improve.

Take a piece that's within your present capabilities and that you've never tried before. Force yourself to play the piece from beginning to end. Keep going, don't stop. Once you stop to correct an error, you've stopped sight-reading and started practicing. Spend a few minutes each day sight-reading, and you'll be surprised how fast you improve, and how much more productive practicing becomes.

First, Browse the Piece

You've chosen material to sight-read. Now what do you do? First, quickly browse over the piece. Check the beginning of the first staff for the key signature and meter, and quickly look over the rest of the piece to judge its level of difficulty. This visual overview will answer technical questions: What sharps or flats are needed? What kind of note gets a beat? What tempo is reasonable for a first reading? Browse the following example and then continue.

Minuet—Treble Clef

Allegretto ♩ = **108**

George Frideric Handel

Minuet—Bass Clef

Allegretto ♩ = **108**

George Frideric Handel

Minuet—Alto Clef

Allegretto ♩ = **108**

George Frideric Handel

Notes, Rhythm, Dynamics, Articulation, Expression Marks: What First?

The First Reading

There's so much to know about a new piece of music—notes, rhythms, articulations, dynamics, expression marks—how much can you expect to get on the first reading? That will depend on the difficulty of the piece. Generally, however, try to get the correct rhythms and notes first.

If the piece is difficult and you must concentrate on either rhythms or notes, go for correct rhythms. If you play an incorrect note and a correct rhythm, you can correct the note later, but you're where you should be in the music. If you play an incorrect rhythm and a correct note, however, the correct note is in the wrong place. A correct note in the wrong place could be a wrong note, because you're not where you should be in the music.

This is an important difference. Sight-reading is part of playing in all musical ensembles. In a group reading situation, if you're in the wrong place, you're lost.

What Next?

If rhythm and notes don't present a problem, then add articulations, followed by dynamics and expression marks. Don't be afraid to read a piece a number of times, adding more depth with each reading. Eventually, you'll be aware of all notated musical directions, and get more of them on the first reading.

Peek Above the First Staff: There's More There than Meets the Eye!

When you get the notes, rhythms, articulations, dynamics and expression marks, congratulations—you've come a long way. You've interpreted the technical symbols. But, what about the musical information? The musical style? How fast should it go? What's the composer trying to express?

This information is also on the music, but it is often ignored. To find the technical information, you looked at the beginning of the first staff. To find the musical information, you must look *above* the first staff.

Check the Center

The title is in the center of the sheet. The title tells a great deal about the character of the music and how it should be interpreted. You would interpret a piece titled *March* in a very different way from one titled *Lullaby* or *Jazz Waltz*.

Minuet (Moderate Waltz Tempo)

Check the Right Side

The composer's name is printed on the right-hand side of the music, just above the first staff. This is important information. The composer indicates the period of music history in which the piece was written. Just as with today's music, each period has its own style. By knowing composers' names, you can find out when they lived. By listening, you have been introduced to period styles, and know how individual styles sound.

Minuet

George Frederic Handel (1685-1759: Baroque)

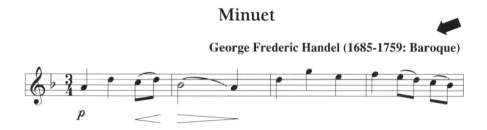

Check The Left Side

The tempo mark is on the left side, above the key and meter signatures. The tempo mark may be a word, such as *allegro,* meaning lively, or *adagio,* meaning slowly. Or, it may be a number that indicates a metronome marking. (See Metronome, Chapter 6.)

Minuet

Allegretto ♩ = *108*

The tempo indications will vary from piece to piece, but all indications convey the composer's or editor's intended tempo. Remember, however, these indications refer to how fast or slow the piece should be performed. For sight-reading, pick a tempo that's comfortable for you.

Now you have the technical and musical information needed to sight-read and think like a musician.

Ear Training

Sight-reading is another way of practicing away from the instrument. (See Chapter 5, "Practicing Away from Your Instrument.") Try looking at a piece and imagining the way it will sound. Imagining the sounds of symbols on the printed page is excellent ear-training. Why not develop your ear along with your technique? Remember the way you think is the way you play!

Auditions

Sight-reading is a standard part of most auditions. How well you sight-read will indicate how much rehearsal time you'll need to perform a piece.

At some point, you'll probably be asked to audition. Whether it's in or outside of school, DO IT! Audition as much as possible! It becomes easier each time.

Auditioning is a wonderful experience. Throughout life you'll have to represent yourself, whether it's giving an oral report in front of your class or going out later in life to take a job interview.

When you audition, you're simply performing for someone. You do it every time you take a lesson or play for your parents. You're simply saying, "Here I am! This is how I perform! I've done my best and I'm proud to show you what I can do!"

Notes

Developing a Balanced Technique

Part V

Your Teacher's Manual: Teaching Tips and Suggestions

10
Teaching Tips

Being Your Own Teacher Means Accepting Responsibility for Your Progress

When you develop musical skills, you're practicing. When you evaluate and guide your own progress, however, you're being your own teacher.

Teachers are also good students. They're constantly learning, but never know how much they understand until they try teaching others.

Being your own teacher is a challenge because you must accept responsibility for your development and challenge yourself to move further ahead. It's a great way to both learn and experience the joys of learning.

Be Patient

Be nice to yourself! Treat yourself the way you would like other teachers to treat you. Be patient, give yourself a pat on the back when you deserve it, and a balanced technique will develop over time. Don't get discouraged when it doesn't happen immediately.

Be Persistent

There'll be times when you feel like you're running in place. You've hit a plateau—a temporary slow down. Be persistent and suddenly you're over it. Like finding that you've outgrown your clothes, it seems to happen all at once. When it happens, however, it's because you've been working at it consistently for a long time.

Recognize Your Strengths

When we evaluate ourselves, too often we only concentrate on what we're doing wrong, and fail to recognize what we're doing right. You may tend to be more critical of yourself than anyone else would be. Evaluate your weaknesses but be sure to give yourself credit for your strengths.

Ask and Answer
Your Own Questions

You'll have to ask yourself questions and answer them to evaluate your progress. Before you can ask questions, however, you need to know what types of questions to ask. The sections that follow contain sample questions you can ask yourself concerning your progress. Use them for starters, and add your own. If you're not sure of an answer, don't be afraid to say, "I don't know." Then research the answer or discuss it with your teacher.

You started by renting your teacher's ears. Now, your answers will help you develop your own.

Review the Basics:
Discover Your Hidden Technique

Technical problems are often caused by flaws in basics. Once corrected, however, you might discover a treasure of skills you already have but may not be aware of. Why go in circles when small adjustments may be all you need? A good teacher looks to these first.

A Picture Is Worth a Thousand Words

Backwards Bob swings. It's a long fly ball to center field. The center fielder moves under it and makes the catch! Can you picture that? Can you picture yourself as the center fielder?

If you want to be a baseball player, you can choose your favorite professional players as models. You know what they look like when they field or hit the ball. If you want to be an actor, you know how actors look in films, television or on the stage. These images help you when you play baseball or take a part in a play. You can picture yourself in your role model's place.

Picture Yourself as a Musician

Picturing yourself as a professional musician can also be helpful. Mental pictures are especially useful when dealing with basics: posture, head position and hand position. Minor corrections in these areas can instantly improve tone quality and intonation and increase flexibility. Checking the basics first can increase confidence, and may help you avoid developing bad performance habits.

Mirror Image

To get the picture, get a picture of a professional musician performing on the instrument you play. Look at the picture—then look at yourself in a mirror. Picture yourself as that professional. Look at other pictures and notice similarities and differences.

As you visualize yourself as the professional, ask yourself:

- Is my posture good?

- Is my head in a normal, comfortable upright position?

- Are my hands relaxed and making proper contact with my instrument?

As you look in the mirror, the answers to these questions are right before your eyes. Let's see what hidden skills these answers may uncover.

Is My Posture Perfect? How Can It Help?

Poor posture is often the cause of inferior tone quality and intonation, breath control problems, lack of flexibility, uneven tone quality between low, middle and high registers, and improper physical contact with the instrument.

How can good posture help? Sit or stand straight and ask yourself:

- Did my tone quality improve?

- Was the intonation more accurate?

- Can I breathe deeper and more comfortably?

- Do I feel more in control?

- Can I change registers more easily?

Is My Head on Straight? How Can that Help?

Even with perfect posture, you may not realize that your head is bending down to meet the instrument. This is common for wind players. The results of poor head position are SIMILAR to those listed above for poor posture.

How can good head position help? Again, sit or stand straight with your head in a normal upright position, listen carefully and ask yourself the questions listed in the previous section. How did you do?

Are My Hands Making Proper Contact with the Instrument?

Music and sports have a great deal in common. Both use quick, relaxed and precise motions. So, for good hand position, relax. Tension in your hands, wrists or arms will slow you down, just as tense muscles will slow down an athlete. Relaxed hand positions lead to a more comfortable and natural contact with the instrument. Remember, your instrument should be a natural extension of you.

How can good hand position help? Relax, make the contact with your instrument as natural as possible, and ask yourself:

- Do I feel any tension in my hands?

- Are my wrists comfortable?

- Are my arms comfortable?

How Often Should I Review Basic Questions?

Review these questions periodically. Habits have habits of their own. They return when least expected.

Overlooked and Often Unasked Basic Questions

Do I Use a Music Stand?

It may be more convenient to put music on a table or on the bed when you practice, but don't! Use a music stand! Whether you're sitting or standing, a music stand can be adjusted to a comfortable height; the table and bed can't. If you have to bend or lean over to read the music, you'll develop bad posture and poor head and hand position. Why develop bad habits when you're working so hard to avoid them? Use a music stand; it's an important practice tool.

Is Everything Working?

You can't cut down a tree with a butter knife, fill a leaking instrument with air or play a rich sound on a worn-out string. Always be sure your instrument and equipment are in good working condition. Take good care of your instrument, and have it checked periodically. If an instrument has slight flaws, you may adjust your playing habits to compensate for these flaws. By doing so, it's easy to develop bad habits as a result of faulty equipment.

No instrument, even one in perfect playing condition, will work properly if reeds, strings, sticks or picks are broken, chipped or worn out. Always have extra replacement equipment in case your instrument requires it.

Can Games and Hobbies Improve My Practicing?

Everybody has favorite games and activities. That's important, keep them up. Stay active and keep yourself in the best possible condition. That way you can enjoy everything you do, practicing included.

Games and hobbies can also make practicing more productive. Wind players and singers, for example, find that games, sports and activities that increase lung capacity will help breath control. Enjoying these and other activities can be an important part of practicing. So run, read, ride your bike, swim!

In short, anything you do that makes you feel physically alive and mentally alert will make practicing more productive.

11

Building a Balanced Technique:
Checklists for Progress

By answering the questions in the previous chapter, you may have discovered hidden skills you didn't realized you had. Now it's time to revisit each area of a balanced technique and to ask yourself specific questions about your progress.

It's a teacher's responsibility to evaluate the progress of students. As your own teacher, it's your responsibility to evaluate yourself.

Use the questions that follow to both evaluate your progress and help plan your practice sessions.

Tone Quality

- ☐ Have I listened to enough music performed on the instrument I play or the voice part I sing to recognize good tone quality?

- ☐ Have I listened to enough music of various styles to recognize that different types of tone qualities are appropriate for different styles of music?

- ☐ Do I like the tone quality I get?

- ☐ Is my tone quality pleasing?

- ☐ Is my tone quality too harsh?

- ☐ Is my tone quality full and rich?

- ☐ Is my tone quality even between registers?

- ☐ Can I vary my tone quality to meet the needs of different styles of music?

Intonation

- ☐ Do I know what good intonation means?

- ☐ Can I hear if I'm playing or singing in tune?

- ☐ Do some pitches sound too high-sharp? or too low-flat?

- ☐ Do I listen for intonation problems when I practice?

- ☐ Can I sing what I want to play?

☐ Can I hear and imagine the sound I want before I play or sing it?

☐ When I perform with other people, do I listen to all the sounds around me to be sure my pitch level fits in?

Breath Control
(For Wind Players and Singers)

☐ Am I breathing correctly?

☐ Is the lower part of my body expanding?

☐ Am I breathing deeply? Is my stomach going out without allowing my chest to rise?

☐ Does my posture allow me to breathe correctly?

☐ Do I have the breath control needed to perform various dynamic levels, ranging from loud (forte) to soft (piano), and still retain good intonation?

☐ Do I pencil in breath marks that match musical phrases?

☐ Do I play or sing long tones to develop good breath control?

☐ Can I use my breath to sustain tones and vary the dynamic level without varying the intonation?

☐ Do my breath and lip formation (embouchure) work as a team?

Finger Control

- ☐ Is my hand position correct?

- ☐ Are my hands, arms and wrists relaxed and free of tension?

- ☐ Do I play scales, chords, and other practice materials slowly at first, and then work up to faster speeds?

- ☐ Do I isolate and repeat more difficult fingering patterns?

- ☐ Do I isolate problem fingerings and work them out slowly?

- ☐ Do I only play a piece or exercise as fast as I can comfortably play the most difficult passage?

- ☐ Do I listen carefully for uneven and difficult fingering connections?

Exercises and Studies

- ☐ Can I read all the note names?

- ☐ Do I understand all the rhythms and rhythm patterns?

- ☐ Do I know all the correct fingerings?

- ☐ Do I know in which scale patterns I should use alternate fingerings?

- ☐ Can I sing what I want to play?

- ☐ Do I read through new exercises by starting slowly and gradually increasing tempo (speed)?

☐ Do I mark in, or think out, the phrasing that makes musical sense?

☐ Can I make music out of exercises?

☐ Do I follow the printed articulations, dynamics and other expression marks?

Articulation (All Musicians)

☐ Can I sing the articulation patterns I want to perform?

☐ Can I hear in my mind, the different ways the same rhythm patterns will sound with various articulations?

☐ Do I work on the more difficult articulation patterns the way I work on more difficult fingerings?

☐ Do I practice scales and exercises in the following basic articulation patterns?

Articulation
(Wind Players)

- ☐ Is my tongue in the proper position?

- ☐ Am I using the tip of my tongue?

- ☐ Is the tip of my tongue making correct contact with the proper area of my mouth or mouthpiece?

- ☐ Do my tongue, breath and fingers work as a team?

- ☐ Do I try different syllables to get different types of tonguing?

Interpretation

- ☐ Do I listen to enough music to know both the joy of listening as well as what different styles of music should sound like?

- ☐ Do I sing the music I want to perform to get the feeling of freedom that comes from not having to consider the technical problems of producing it?

- ☐ Do I put myself and the way I feel into the music?

- ☐ Do I try singing, then performing, the same piece or exercise different ways until I find the one that I like?

☐ Do I use dynamics and expression marks to vary the mood of the music?

☐ **Does the music come alive for me?**

Remember, the end result of your practicing is to enjoy music. Whether you use your skills to perform classical music, rock, jazz, folk, country, gospel, new age or any other style, the technical skills you must develop are the same. The only difference is how you use them.

Discuss these questions with your parents, teachers and friends. They may have additional suggestions.

Practice Habits Relate to Daily Life

If you've become your own teacher of music, why not be your own teacher in other areas as well? Good practice habits are no different from good study and learning habits in other areas. If you practice in a well-organized manner, apply those techniques and skills to other interests and subjects.

What you've learned isn't limited to music. You've learned to use your time wisely. You've learned how to pace yourself. Most of all, as your own teacher, you've learned to take the responsibility for your own learning and development.

In short, you've gained the satisfaction and confidence that come from a job well done. With these organizational skills, you can accomplish anything you want in less time and with more enjoyment. Whether you're trying to solve a mathematics problem, learn about stamp collecting, run a computer or become a better baseball player, it doesn't matter: you trust yourself and have the confidence that you can do it.

When you're asked, "How did you accomplish so much?" you can smile proudly and reply, "I knew what I wanted to do, I worked hard and consistently at it, but most of all—*I had a good teacher—ME!*

Notes

Becoming My Own Teacher

Index

A
Accent, 107
Articulation, 87, 105–108
Articulation checklist, 137–138
Auditions, 120–121

B
Backwards Bob, 5, 7, 8, 9, 12, 22, 35, 52, 127
Balanced technique, 89–110
Balanced technique, checklists, 133–138
Baseball, 5, 11, 12, 83, 84, 86, 92
Basics, review of, 127–132
Beethoven, 98, 99
Being in tune, 66–67, 96
Being musical, 86
Bow, 66, 86, 93, 106
Breath control, 42, 106, 129, 132
Breath control checklist, 135

C
CD ROMs, 77–78
Chocolate cake, 18, 19, 90
Clapping, 40, 58
Classical music, 68, 75, 102, 104, 105, 139
Commitment, 11
Computer, 69, 74–77, 112
Concentration, 9, 35, 41, 60, 94
Concept of sound, 18–20
Confidence, 8, 9, 23, 24, 52, 54, 100, 128, 139
Consistency, 51, 52, 92
Country music, 68, 75, 139
Crescendo, 110

D

Dead sound, 40
Decisions, 37–40
Diminuendo, 110
Drumsticks, 42, 66, 86, 93, 106, 132
Dynamic marks, 109
Dynamics, 87, 108–110

E

Ears, developing yours, 17, 18, 20, 41, 53, 59, 96, 120
Evaluating your progress, 125, 126, 133
Exercise checklist, 136–137
Expression marks, 117

F

Faulty equipment, 132
Feelings, 8, 21, 85, 94, 108
Finger control, 54, 66, 87, 96–105, 106
Finger control checklist, 136
Flexibility, 95, 128, 129
FM radio, 68–69
Folk music, 139
Frustration, 4, 13, 61

G

Game of music, 85, 112
Games, 132
Gospel music, 105, 139

H

Habits, 12, 35, 41, 42, 48, 51, 56, 59, 61, 130
Hand position, 42, 128, 130
Handel, George Frideric, 116, 118, 119
Happy Harry, 6, 7, 8, 17, 23, 38, 97
Hard work and patience, 61
Head position, 128, 129–130
History, 85, 86

Hobbies, 132
Homework, 14, 15, 49

I

Ice cream, 90
Improvisation, 75, 102, 103, 104, 112
Interpretation, 69, 87, 111–114
Interpretation checklist, 138
Intonation, 19, 53, 54, 67, 87, 92, 93, 100, 110, 128, 129
Intonation checklist, 134–135

J

Jazz, 68, 75, 102, 105

L

Legato attack, 107
Lessons, 9, 10, 16, 17, 57, 59
Listening, 17, 18, 19, 20, 22, 41, 54, 56, 66, 68, 69, 94, 95, 96, 101, 102,
    109, 112, 113, 119
Live sound, 40, 41
Long tones, 95

M

Malzel, 64, 65
Manuscript paper, 41
Mathematics, 14, 15, 16, 49
Metronome, 64–66, 69
Mezzo forte, 109–110
Mind, 34, 53, 91, 113
Mirror, 42, 128, 129
Module, sound, 75, 76
Mother Nature, 100–101
Mozart, 98
Music history, 70, 97, 112
Music reading, 58
Music stand, 41, 69, 131
Music theory, 70, 112

Photo Credits

Page 25, left, Artley piccolos, courtesy of United Musical Instruments U.S.A., Inc., Elkhart, IN 46516.

Page 25, top right, Holton trombone, courtesy of G. Leblanc Corporation, Kenosha, WI 53141-1415.

Page 25, bottom right, Corona II accordion, courtesy of Hohner, Inc., Richmond, VA 23227-0435.

Page 26, top left, Selmer tenor and alto saxophones, courtesy of Selmer, Elkhart, IN 46516.

Page 26, bottom left, Steinway grand piano, courtesy of Steinway & Sons, Long Island City, NY 11105.

Page 26, top right, Conn French Horn, courtesy of United Musical Instruments U.S.A., Inc., Elkhart IN 46516.

Page 26, bottom right, Armstrong oboe, courtesy of United Musical Instruments U.S.A., Inc., Elkhart, IN 46516.

Page 27, top left, Conn baritone horn, courtesy of United Musical Instruments U.S.A., Inc., Elkhart, IN 46516.

Page 27, middle left, Bach trumpet, courtesy of Selmer, Elkhart, IN 46516.

Page 27, bottom, Yamaha W5 synthesizer, courtesy of Yamaha Corporation of America, Buena Park, CA 90622-6600.

Page 27, left, Artley Bassoon, courtesy of United Musical Instruments U.S.A., Inc., Elkhart, IN 46516.

Page 28, left, Selmer clarinet, courtesy of Selmer, Elkhart, IN 46516.

Page 28, top right, Marine Band harmonica, courtesy of Hohner, Inc., Richmond, VA 23227-0435.

Page 28, middle right, PureCussion drum set, courtesy of PureCussion, Minneapolis, MN 55416.

Page 28, bottom right, Scherl & Roth violin, courtesy of United Musical Instruments U.S.A., Inc., Elkhart, IN 46516.

Page 29, top left, Robert Cray Strat electric guitar, courtesy of Fender Musical Instruments Corp., Scottsdale, AZ 85258.

Page 29, bottom left, Conn song flute, courtesy of United Musical Instruments U.S.A., Inc., Elkhart, IN 46516.

Page 29, right, Getzen marching mellophone, courtesy of Getzen Company, Elkhorn, WI 53121.

Page 39, Selmer flute, courtesy of Selmer, Elkhart, IN 46516.

Page 65, left, Franz Keywound Metronome, right, Franz Quartz Electric Integrated Metronome, courtesy of Franz Manufacturing Company, Inc., New Haven, CT 06512.

Page 67, Yamaha electronic tuner, courtesy of Yamaha Corporation of America, Buena Park, CA 90622-6600.

Page 71, top, "You Can Sing, " bottom, "Mastering the Electric Bass," courtesy of Homespun Tapes, Woodstock, NY 12498.

Page 72, top left, "Fiddle for Kids" and top right "Jack Dejohnette," courtesy of Homespun Tapes, Woodstock, NY 12498.

Page 72, bottom left, illustration from *The Reed Maker's Manual and The Reed Maker's Video*, published by David B. Weber and Ferald Capps, courtesy of Weber Reeds, P.O. Box 59741, Birmingham, AL 35259-9741, (205) 870-0284.

Page 73, top, "Easy Guitar Maintenance and Repair," courtesy of Homespun Tapes, Woodstock, NY 12498.

Page 73, bottom, "Finding Your Way with Hand Drums," courtesy of Interworld Music, Brattleboro, VT 05301.

Page 74, "Symbol Simon," courtesy of Electronic Courseware Systems, Inc., Champaign, IL 61821.

Page 75, "Music Ace," courtesy of Harmonic Vision, Evanston, IL 60201.

Page 76, top, Yamaha W7 music synthesizer, bottom, Yamaha tone generator, courtesy of Yamaha Corporation of America, Buena Park, CA 90620.

Page 77, notation software, courtesy of Mark of the Unicorn, Cambridge, MA 02138.

Page 131, music stands, courtesy of Hamilton Stands Inc., Monroe, OH 45050.

About the Author

Dr. Snitkin teaches at Three Rivers Community Technical College, is a consultant with Music and Music Education Services, and has been an educator and musician for over thirty years. He holds a Ph.D. in Music Education (Supervision and Curriculum Development), an M.A. in Oboe Pedagogy from the University of Connecticut, and a Bachelor of Music Education from the Hartt College of Music.

Dr. Snitkin has taught all levels of public school music as well as at the Hartt School of Music, the Armed Forces School of Music, and the University of Connecticut. He has been coordinator of numerous arts education grants and served for over twenty-five years as music director of the Eastern Connecticut Symphony Youth Orchestra.

He is a two-time recipient of the Connecticut Songwriter Association's "Contribution to Education Through Music Award."

Dr. Snitkin is a member of the MENC, the National Academy of Recording Arts and Sciences (a voting member for the Grammy Awards), an associate composer of Broadcast Music International (his songs are recorded on Steljo Records), and the author of the *Reed Player's Series* (HMS Publications, Inc.) for oboe, bassoon and single-reeds.